Fresh, Fast and Fabulous

A collection of simple, satisfying meals from Sam's Club® Members and culinary partners

Welcome to the second edition of *Fresh, Fast and Fabulous.* The response to our first cookbook was so enthusiastic, it inspired a repeat performance! While this collection is filled with all-new recipes, helpful tips and unique entertaining ideas, you'll find that variety with a focus on simplicity has remained the same. Designed for minimum fuss and maximum enjoyment, most dishes can be made with just eight ingredients or less, available at your local Sam's Club. And for every great meal you'll find the best ingredients, because our buyers travel the world to bring the highest-quality hand-cut meats, premium seafood and the freshest, most flavorful produce—all with a generous helping of value—to your table. Thank you for making Sam's Club part of the family. Your loyalty and support are at the heart of this book. We hope you'll turn to it often for everyday meals and special occasions alike.

For additional nutritional information and more, visit **SamsClub.com/meals**.

Sam's Club Advertised Merchandise Policy - It is our firm intention to have every advertised item in stock. Occasionally, however, an advertised item may not be available for purchase due to unforeseen difficulties. We reserve the right to limit quantities to normal retail purchases or one-per-Member or household, and to exclude resellers. We have done our best to ensure all information in this piece is accurate and up-to-date. Errors and omissions occasionally occur and are subject to correction. Quantities may be limited on select items. Pricing and item availability may vary by location and in Hawaii and Alaska. All trademarks are property of their respective owners. Unless otherwise noted, prices for items ordered at **SamsClub.com** do not include shipping costs.

At Sam's Club, we provide safe, quality food at exceptional savings to our Members. Because we care about your safety, we would like to remind you of the importance of following proper food safety practices. Please visit **foodsafety.gov/keep/index.html** to view safe handling procedures, cooking temperatures and food safety tips for you and your family.

Consult your medical professional for guidance before changing or undertaking a new diet or exercise program. Advance consultation with your physician is particularly important if you are under eighteen (18) years old, pregnant, nursing or have health problems. If you have dietary restrictions and/or allergies, always read the ingredient list carefully for all food products prior to consumption. Allergens and their derivatives can have various names and may be present in some food brands but not others. If the ingredient list is not available on the food product, check with the food manufacturer or do not consume the product. If you have a food allergy, speak to your physician and/or a registered dietitian for a comprehensive list of foods and their derivatives to avoid prior to using any recipe provided by Sam's Club. Neither the author nor Sam's Club assumes any responsibility for errors, omissions or contrary interpretation of the subject matter herein.

Recipe development on Pages 73, 75, 76, 77, 78, 79, 80 and 81 by Mike Chapter and Elizabeth Nelson.
Recipe development on Pages 72, 74, 77, 79 and 81 by Troy Black.
Recipe development on Pages 122-123 by Erin Quon and Kristen Butler.
Making It Simple Tips provided by and supplier recipes tested by Linda Hall.

SECOND EDITION

All recipe photography by Manny Rodriguez Photography, Dallas, TX.

Pictured on the front cover (clockwise from top left): San Diego Cheeseburgers (Page 35), Seafood Marinade with a Kick (Page 77), New Zealand Rack of Lamb with Grilled Red Pepper-almond Sauce (Page 68), Patriotic Tea Punch (Page 121).

Pictured on the back cover (left to right, top to bottom): Cranberry-chili Meatballs (Page 28), Maple-glazed Chicken with Waldorf Salsa (Page 42), Chilled Hunt's® Tomato and Vegetable Pasta Salad (Page 84), Citrus Marinade (Page 73), Bubbly Berries with Lemon Sorbet (Page 108) and Summer Cranberry Spritzer (Page 120).

Printed in China.

Making it simple:

Fuss-free food prep and storage ideas from the Sam's Club® Kitchens

Marinate like a pro: A marinade can help make meat tender and lend flavor to everything you grill. Here are some guidelines for how long to marinate for best results:

• Chicken: ½ hour to 2 hours
• Fish: 15 to 60 minutes
• Tender meats: 1 to 2 hours
• Less tender cuts: 2 hours to overnight

Always marinate foods in the refrigerator, and never leave out at room temperature or reuse marinade.

Get it ripe: Did you know that bananas give off the gas that helps other fruit ripen? Simply place peaches, pears or other fruit that needs softening in a paper bag with a banana in it. You'll enjoy sweet success in no time at all.

Berry smart: It's easy to enjoy that bounty of berries from Sam's Club anytime! Gently rinse and pat dry, then arrange on a cookie sheet without touching and freeze uncovered until solid. Carefully remove with a metal spatula and transfer to an airtight container. Store in freezer, and use as needed for smoothies, desserts, or as mini ice cubes in summer drinks.

Spud sense: For a creamy texture and more even cooking, start potatoes in cold water first, then bring to a boil. Leave skins on to lend natural color and extra nutrients.

It's easy being green: Love guacamole but hate when it turns brown? Keep it looking as fresh as it takes by covering the bowl with plastic wrap and pressing directly onto the surface to seal completely. This helps to protect it from exposure to air, which causes the change in color. Serve with your favorite chips, as a side with Mexican food, and as a topping on the zesty San Diego Cheeseburgers (find the recipe on Page 35).

Make it simple on yourself: When entrées and side dishes are the focus of your summer entertaining, choose appetizers and desserts that serve themselves: chips and salsa, fresh-cut fruits and veggies, and Mediterranean favorites like olives and roasted peppers are great starters that can hold up for a few hours. Sundae bars are a fun, no-prep dessert. You provide the ice cream and toppings, let the guests create their personal perfect endings.

Build a Better Burger:
The best-tasting burgers start with the best ingredients. Sam's Club ground beef makes an excellent choice. Customize by personal preference or occasion with your favorite seasonings, chopped fresh herbs, shredded cheese and more, worked gently into the meat to avoid toughness.

Ground Beef:
Choose 80% lean chuck for the most flavorful burgers. Shape patties ½" thick and place burgers on a hot grill or skillet. Turn occasionally and avoid pressing down to keep them juicy.

Ground Turkey:
To keep turkey burgers or meatloaves moist, mix a small amount of barbecue sauce, mayonnaise or an egg into the meat before cooking.

Top it off:
Be creative! Go Hawaiian with pineapple and Swiss cheese, zesty with salsa and dollops of guacamole and sour cream, or feta cheese, black olives and onions. Swap out hamburger buns for ciabatta rolls, pita, English muffins or croissants for a delicious change of pace.

Making the Cut: We know you'll love our beef, USDA Choice or above, because it's specially selected and hand-cut for flavor and tenderness by meat experts. And it's all backed by our 200% freshness guarantee.

recipe on **pg. 54**

Strip Steak:
This boneless steak (also called New York Strip) is the perfect size for one person. Try grilling and slicing onto salads or in sandwiches.

How to cook: Cook quickly over medium heat on the grill or in a skillet on the stove. Let rest at least 5 minutes before slicing.

recipe on **pg. 38**

Top Sirloin Steak:
Extremely versatile, this steak is great for marinating. Its larger size gives you multiple portions for stir-frys, sandwiches or skewers.

How to cook: Slice into thin strips for stir-frying, cut into 1" pieces for kabobs or grill whole steaks on medium heat.

Ribeye Steak:
This boneless cut is super tender and full of flavor. Serve individually or slice for salads, wraps or sandwiches.

How to cook: Ribeyes cook quickly, either on the grill, under the broiler or in a skillet. Avoid high heat—medium ensures even cooking.

Flank Steak:
This lean steak is perfect for marinating. It makes great fajitas, sandwiches and kabobs.

How to cook: Slice thinly across the grain for skillet cooking. Marinate up to 24 hours for grilling over medium heat or broiling.

Top Round: Because it is so lean, Top Round (often called London Broil) is less tender and benefits from marinating. Always slice thinly against the grain for maximum tenderness.

How to cook: Marinate up to 24 hours. Grill or broil whole steaks and avoid overcooking.

Bone-in Short Ribs: Full of flavor, these ribs benefit from long, slow cooking rather than barbecuing. A great comfort dish for cooler weather.

How to cook: Cook covered in the oven with at least 1" of liquid (braising) or grill over low flame until crisp on the outside, nicely tender on the inside.

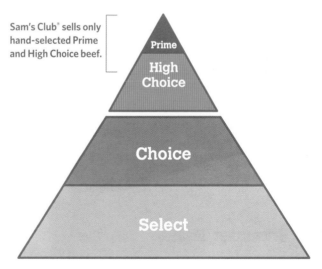

Sam's Club® sells only hand-selected Prime and High Choice beef.

Prime
High Choice
Choice
Select

Brisket: Brisket needs long, slow cooking with moist heat for maximum tenderness. Goes well with barbecue sauce on sandwiches, or braise with cabbage and potatoes for a classic dish.

How to cook: Braise on the grill in a tightly covered foil pan to infuse a great smoky flavor. Can also be prepared in a slow cooker with your favorite sauce or flavorful liquids like fruit or tomato juice.

According to the U.S. Department of Agriculture standards, only the top 50% of all beef is graded Choice and only 2% is graded Prime.

recipe on **pg. 33**

Boneless Pork Tenderloin: Cut into medallions
for sautéing, strips for stir-frying, cubes for kabobs, or cook whole.
Be careful to avoid overcooking to maintain juiciness.

How to cook: Use a spice rub or marinate for flavor. Roast whole in the
oven or grill on medium heat. For skillet cooking, use a small amount of
oil and cook quickly.

Pork Back Ribs: Also called "baby backs," these barbecue-
friendly ribs are small and easy to eat. Apply sauce during the last 10 or
15 minutes of cooking to avoid burning.

How to cook: Pat dry with paper towels before grilling over indirect
medium heat. Keep grill covered to maintain even heat and cook slowly
until very tender.

recipe on **pg. 68**

Pork Shoulder Butts: Sometimes called Boston butt or
picnic shoulder, this cut is perfect for slow roasting, stews and classic
pulled pork sandwiches. Available with or without the bone.

How to cook: Use the "low and slow" method, either on the grill for
several hours (indirect heat) or braised in the oven. Cut into chunks for
stews and brown the meat before adding liquid.

Rack of Lamb: An entire rack can be roasted whole or cut
into individual chops for quick cooking.

How to cook: Sear the meat on all sides in a Dutch oven before roasting
whole, or grill the rack over indirect heat. Individual chops can be grilled
or sautéed in a skillet and are best served rare or medium-rare.

recipe on **pg. 62**

Tuna: Purchase fresh tuna steaks that are deep red and firm to the touch, with the smell of the ocean. Frozen individual tuna steaks provide portion control and easy preparation. Thaw in the refrigerator overnight.

How to cook: Grill or sauté over medium-high heat and serve medium to medium-rare for best flavor and texture. Try quickly searing in a hot pan, then slicing for salads, tacos or sandwiches.

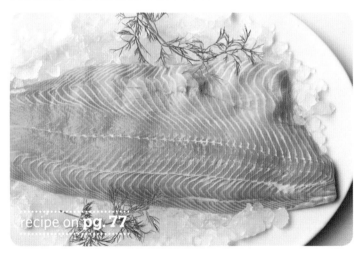

recipe on **pg. 77**

recipe on **pg. 76**

Salmon: Fresh fillets are great for roasting or grilling. They can also be poached, broiled or sautéed.

How to cook: Try a lightly oiled cedar plank when grilling a whole side of this flavorful fish. Salmon is also excellent baked whole or pan-cooked for a healthy salad topper. Keep moist by cooking until it just begins to flake with a fork.

Shrimp: Shrimp size is based on the number of shrimp in each pound. The smaller the number, the larger the shrimp. For example, 31/40 shrimp have 31 to 40 shrimp per pound. Frozen shrimp work well in many recipes and can be thawed quickly. Shrimp marked "U-15" ("U" stands for under) requires fewer than 15 shrimp to make up a pound.

How to cook: Leave shells on for added flavor when boiling. Peeled and deveined shrimp are a fast fix for soups, casseroles, and grilled on skewers. You know they're done when they turn firm and pink.

Food Safety Tips:
Cooking meats and seafood to the recommended internal temperature is one of the best ways to guard against foodborne illness. But proper food safety begins long before you start cooking and continues after you've eaten. Take a look at our tips for keeping your food safe and your family and friends healthy.

Keep your cool: Buy meats, seafood and other temperature-sensitive foods toward the end of your grocery visit. Carry an insulated bag with you or pack a cooler in the car, especially during warm weather.

Have a picnic: If you're planning a picnic, consider bringing one cooler for raw meats that will be grilled and one cooler for cooked foods, salads and drinks. Pack hand sanitizer and disposable wipes if running water isn't available.

Four-hour rule: Always keep hot foods hot and cold foods cold. If that's not possible, a good rule of thumb is allowing foods to remain at room temperature for no more than 4 hours.

Chill out: Soups, stews and casseroles that are freshly cooked can stay hot for quite a while. Before storing, allow them to cool for 1 to 2 hours on the countertop. This will prevent the hot food from raising the temperature of your refrigerator.

Freeze and save, safely: Buying meat in bulk packs and then freezing is a great way to eat well and save money. After purchase, divide meat into meal-sized portions and pack in sturdy resealable or vacuum-sealed bags. Don't forget to include the date! Uncooked meats stored at 0°F generally retain their quality for at least 4 months.

Thaw smart: Never thaw frozen foods on the countertop. The safest method: thaw overnight in the refrigerator. Short on time? Place a sealed package under cool running water (never hot water) or use the defrost setting of your microwave, checking frequently.

Temperature's rising: A digital or instant-read thermometer is a small investment to ensure that food is cooked through and to prevent foodborne illness. Always insert the metal tip into the thickest part of the meat to avoid touching bone or fat. Check in several places to confirm even cooking. Wash thoroughly with warm, soapy water after each use.

Cutting board care: A quality cutting board protects counters and knives from damage during food prep. These simple tips will help ensure food safety and long use:

- Wood: Avoid soaking or submerging in water. Wipe with warm, soapy water to clean; a mild vinegar and water solution helps remove odors. Store upright in a dry place between uses.

- Plastic or synthetic: Wash immediately after use with hot, soapy water or in the dishwasher to prevent staining. Make sure to replace if surface becomes scarred with knife cuts.

Whichever type you choose, never cut raw meat or seafood on the same board as fruits and vegetables. Rubbing the surface with white vinegar helps sanitize and prevent cross-contamination.

Cooking Safety Chart

All temperatures are in degrees Fahrenheit

Product	Type	Internal Temperature (°F)
Beef & Veal	Ground	160
	Steak and roasts –medium	160
	Steak and roasts –medium rare	145
Chicken & Turkey	Breasts	165
	Ground, stuffing and casseroles	165
	Whole bird, legs, thighs and wings	165
Fish & Shellfish	Any type	145
Lamb	Ground	160
Leftovers	Steak and roasts –medium	160
	Steaks and roasts –medium rare	145
	Any type	165
Pork	Chops, fresh (raw) ham ground, ribs and roasts	145
	Fully cooked ham (to reheat)	140

Source: http://www.fsis.usda.gov/Fact_Sheets/Keep_Food_Safe_Food_Safety_Basics/index.asp

For information purposes only. For more information, contact the USDA, FoodSafety.gov or your local and state health departments.

Small Bites, Big Flavor

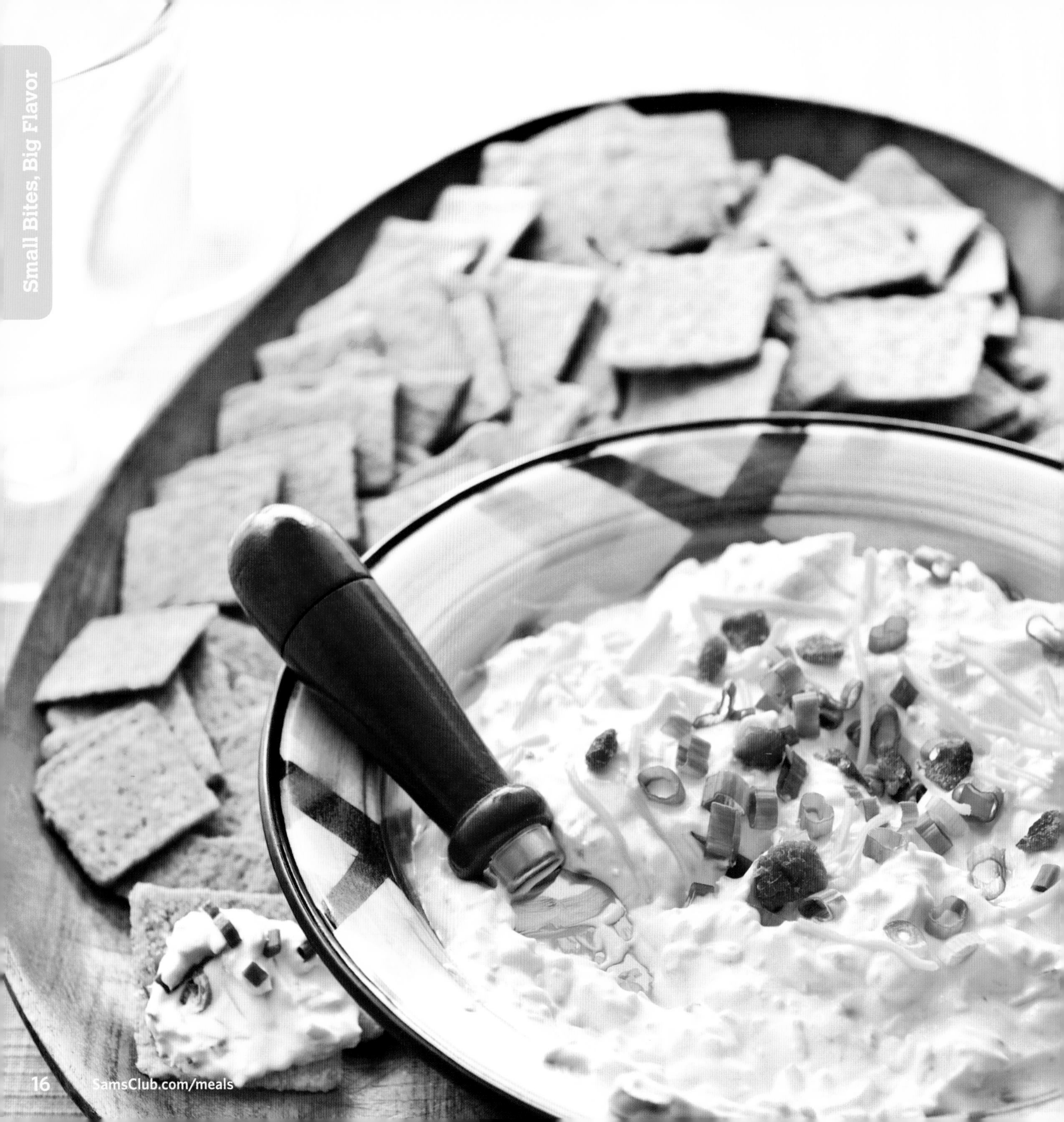

Bacon-cheddar Dip

Savory with a hint of real bacon, this dip is super snackable and simple to make.

Total time: 1 hour, 10 minutes | Makes 18 servings

Ingredients:

2 cups sour cream

1 cup KRAFT® Mexican Style Finely
Shredded Four Cheese

4 slices bacon, cooked and crumbled

2 green onions, sliced

Wheat Thins® Big Snack Crackers

Instructions:

• Mix all ingredients except crackers.

• Refrigerate 1 hour.

• Serve with crackers.

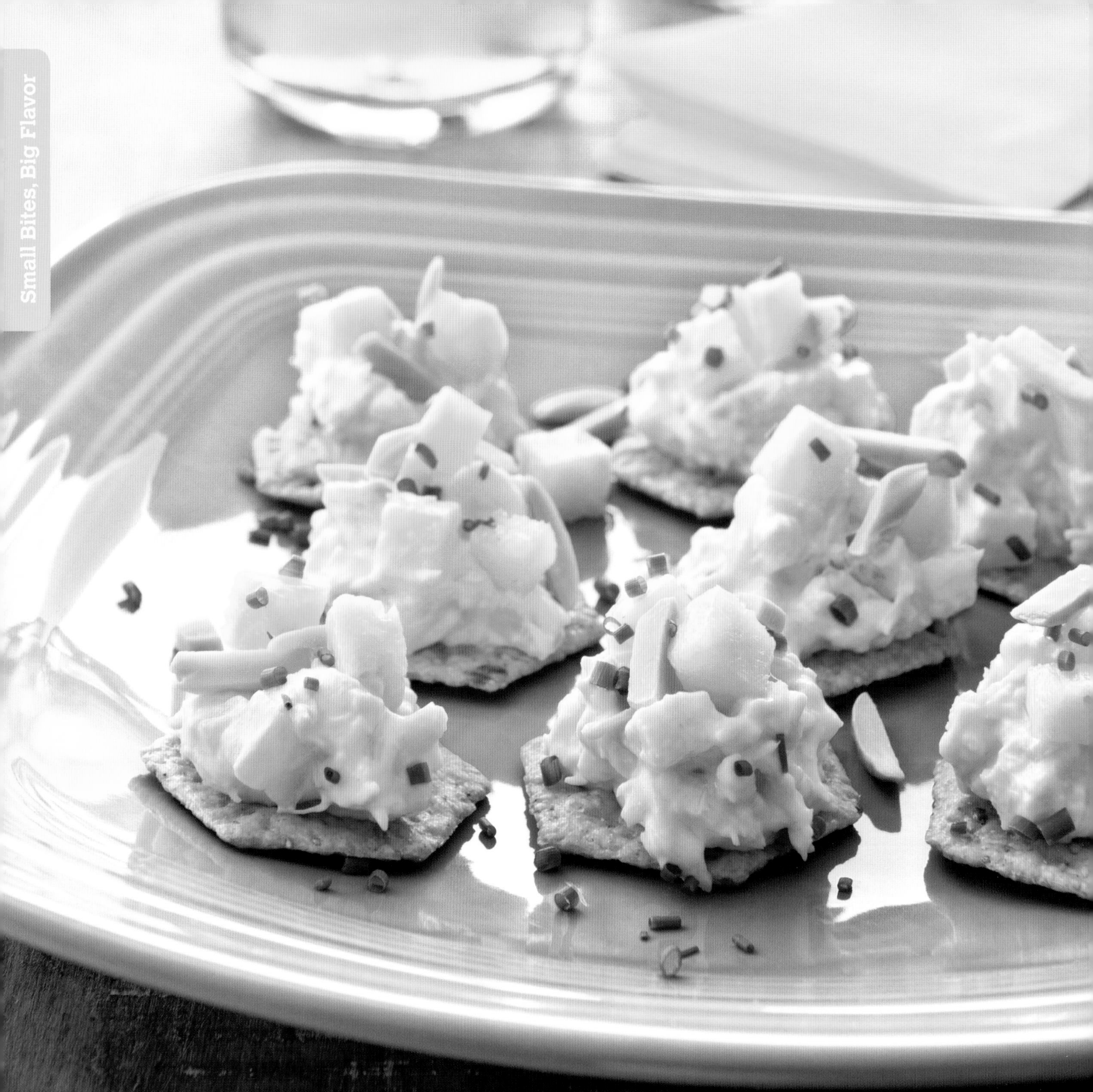

Pineapple-chicken Bites

Say aloha to the everyday with these bite-sized tastes of the tropics.

Total time: 20 minutes | Makes 24 appetizers

Ingredients:

5 oz. chunk chicken, drained and flaked

2 Tbsp. (1 oz.) cream cheese, softened

2 Tbsp. mayonnaise

1 can (20 oz.) DOLE® Pineapple Chunks, drained

2 Tbsp. almonds, chopped

24 small round crackers

Instructions:

• Combine chicken, cream cheese and mayonnaise in medium bowl, mixing well. Chill, if desired, until ready to serve.

• Measure 1 cup drained pineapple chunks; stir into chicken mixture with almonds. Spoon mixture onto crackers; serve.

Store remaining pineapple chunks in refrigerator in a glass or plastic container. Pineapple chunks can be grilled, served over frozen yogurt and salads, or placed on skewers with other delicious fruits like strawberries, mango chunks and peach slices.

Coca-Cola® Chicken Wings

Everyone's favorite soft drink is the secret ingredient in these sweet and tangy wings.

Total time: 2 hours, 10 minutes | Makes 2-4 servings

Ingredients:

1 cup brown sugar

1 can (12 oz.) Coca-Cola®

2 medium onions, chopped

2 cloves garlic, minced

2 Tbsp. soy sauce

Salt and pepper, to taste

3 lbs. chicken wings

Instructions:

• In a large casserole dish or 9x12" pan, combine the brown sugar, Coca-Cola, onions, garlic, soy sauce, salt and pepper. Stir until mixed. Place chicken wings in sauce mixture.

• Bake at 350°F for 2 hours.

• Remove the chicken from the pan, pour sauce into a sauce pan or skillet. Place ¼ cup of the liquid into a small bowl; stir in 2 tablespoons of cornstarch, then return that mixture to the pan. Bring to a boil and pour over the chicken wings.

prep time: **10 min.**

Cowboys' Queso

A deliciously beefed-up version of the classic Mexican cheese dip.

Total time: 1 hour | Makes 6⅓ cups

Ingredients:

1 lb. ground beef

1 pkg. (32 oz.) Velveeta®, cut up

1.25 oz. taco seasoning

1 Tbsp. sour cream

1 Tbsp. butter

1 Tbsp. cream cheese

1 can (10 oz.) RO-TEL® Original Diced Tomatoes & Green Chiles, undrained

1 can (10 oz.) RO-TEL® Original Diced Tomatoes & Green Chiles, drained

Instructions:

• Brown meat in large skillet; drain. Add to slow cooker with all remaining ingredients.

• Cook on low heat 1 hour or until melted, stirring occasionally.

Recipe submitted by:
Heather Allen
Aubrey, TX
Member since 2009

There was a contest for free (Dallas) Cowboys tickets and I won with this recipe. Now we make it for every game, and anytime we have a party.

Fiesta Dip

Cool, creamy and colorful, this dip is numero uno with hungry guests.

Total time: 10 minutes | Makes 16 servings

Ingredients:

1 pkg. (8 oz.) cream cheese, softened

⅓ cup milk

1 oz. Hidden Valley® Salad Dressing & Seasoning Mix

½ cup thick and chunky salsa, medium

2.5 oz. whole black olives, drained, rinsed and coarsely chopped

¼ cup of green onions, sliced

Instructions:

• Blend the cream cheese, milk and dressing in a food processor or with an electric mixer until smooth.

• Stir in salsa, olives and onions, blending well.

• Chill at least one hour. Serve with tortilla chips or vegetables for dipping.

For even more of a kick, stir in ⅛ tsp. of ground red pepper.

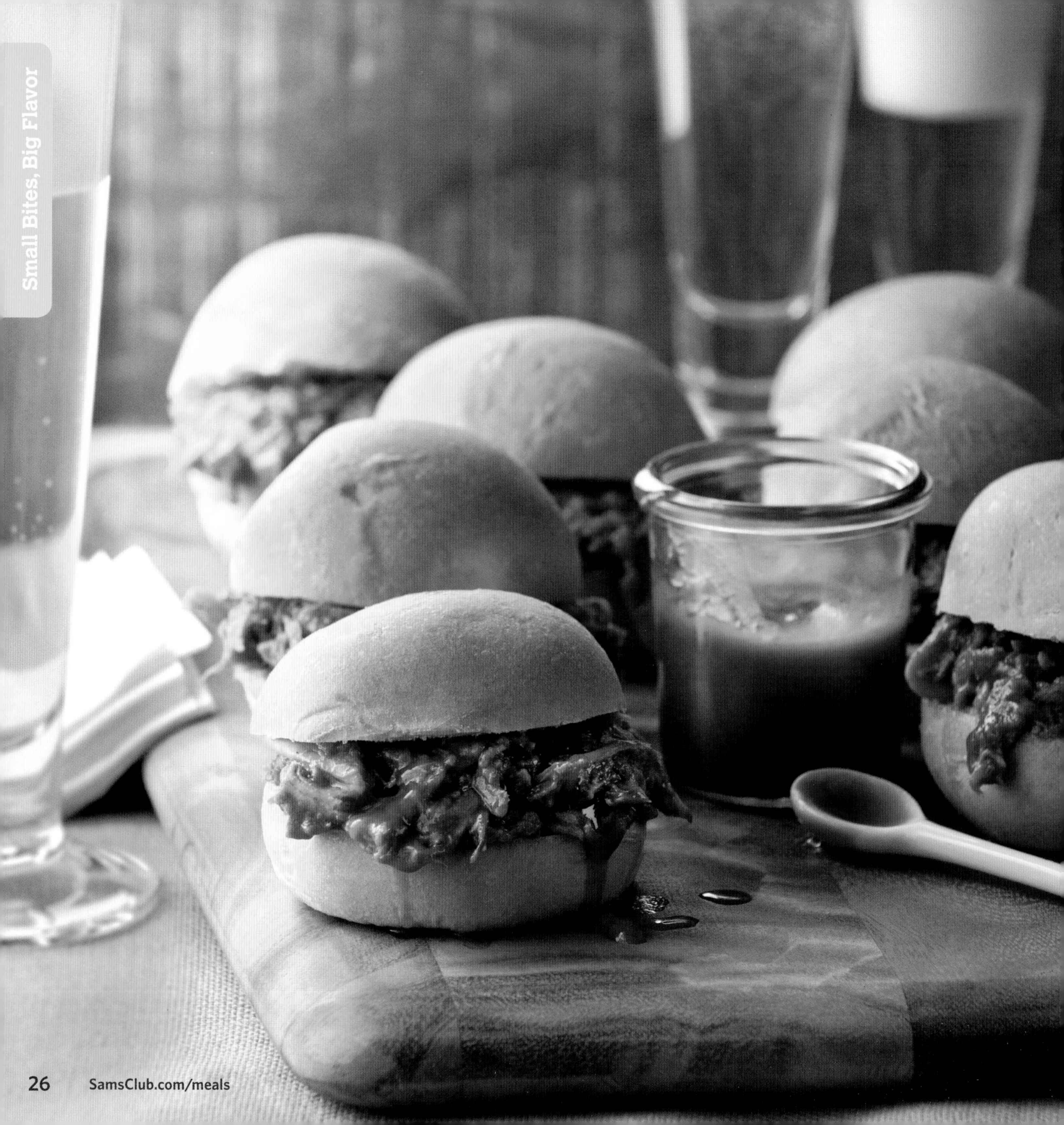

Barbecue Pork Sliders

These little sandwiches are a big hit with barbecue lovers of all ages.

Total time: 1 hour | Makes 30 servings

Ingredients:

4 lbs. Byron's Fully Cooked Pulled Pork Barbecue

60 mini hamburger buns or dinner rolls

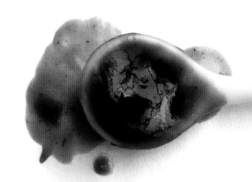

Instructions:

• Preheat oven to 350°F. Heat barbecue tray according to package
instructions, or place thawed product in slow cooker and heat on high for 3 to 4 hours.

• Spoon about 2 tablespoons barbecue onto each roll and serve warm.

*If you can't find mini hamburger buns,
dinner rolls are just as delicious.*

Cranberry-chili Meatballs

A new twist on a classic, with the tangy kick of cranberry.

Total time: 4 hours | Makes 32 servings

Recipe submitted by:

Ann LaCute
Daytona Beach, FL
Member since 1991

Sam's Club® meatballs make it easy. That's why I like it so much. People love it and keep asking for it. So I was glad when they brought in the meatballs to the frozen foods section. I make just a little twist with the ingredients.

Ingredients:

1 jar (12 oz.) chili sauce

1 can jellied cranberry sauce

½ cup brown sugar

½ cup lemon juice

1 bag (96 oz.) Casa Di Bertacchi® Frozen Italian Style Meatballs

Instructions:

• Combine chili sauce, cranberry sauce, brown sugar and lemon juice in slow cooker and stir to combine.

• Add meatballs and stir.

• Cook on low heat 4 hours (or cook on high heat 2½ hours), stirring occasionally.

prep time: 5 min.

Warm Weather Entrées

prep time: **20 min.**

Grilled Pork Tenderloin with Tomato Salad and Fresh Mint

Zesty grilled meat and spicy cool salad are a healthy combination that's bursting with flavor.

Total time: 4 hours, 5 minutes *(includes marinating)* | Makes 8 servings

Ingredients:

Pork
2 pork tenderloins (about 1 lb. ea.)
3 Tbsp. curry powder
1 Tbsp. ground cumin
Juice of ½ lime
¼ cup extra-virgin olive oil
¼ tsp. sea salt
¼ tsp. freshly ground pepper

Tomato Salad
Juice of 1 lime
¼ cup extra-virgin olive oil
½ tsp. sea salt
½ tsp. freshly ground pepper
1 jalapeño chile, including seeds, cut into paper-thin rounds
2½ lbs. vine-ripened tomatoes, quartered
½ small red onion, cut into paper-thin wedges
⅓ cup fresh mint leaves, loosely packed

Instructions:

• To prepare pork, in a small bowl, stir together curry powder, cumin, lime juice, olive oil, salt and pepper to make a paste. Place pork in a small glass baking dish and spread curry mixture over tenderloins to cover completely. Cover and refrigerate for 2 hours.

• While the pork is marinating, make the tomato salad. In a small bowl, combine lime juice, olive oil, salt, pepper and jalapeño. In a large bowl, combine tomatoes, red onion and mint. Stir dressing and pour it over the tomato mixture. Mix gently to combine. Cover and set aside at room temperature until ready to serve.

• Remove pork from the refrigerator. Place a large grill pan on two burners over medium-high heat or preheat an outdoor gas or charcoal grill. Fold a few paper towels into a thick square. Blot some oil on the paper towels and then carefully and quickly wipe the ridges of the grill pan or the hot grates of the grill to make a nonstick surface.

• Put the pork on the grill and cook, turning to brown all sides, for 20 minutes until the center is rosy and the internal temperature reads 145°F when tested with an instant-read thermometer. Transfer to carving board and let rest for 5 minutes.

• To serve, slice pork tenderloin on a slight bias into 1" thick pieces and arrange on plates. Toss salad and pile tomato salad on the side.

33

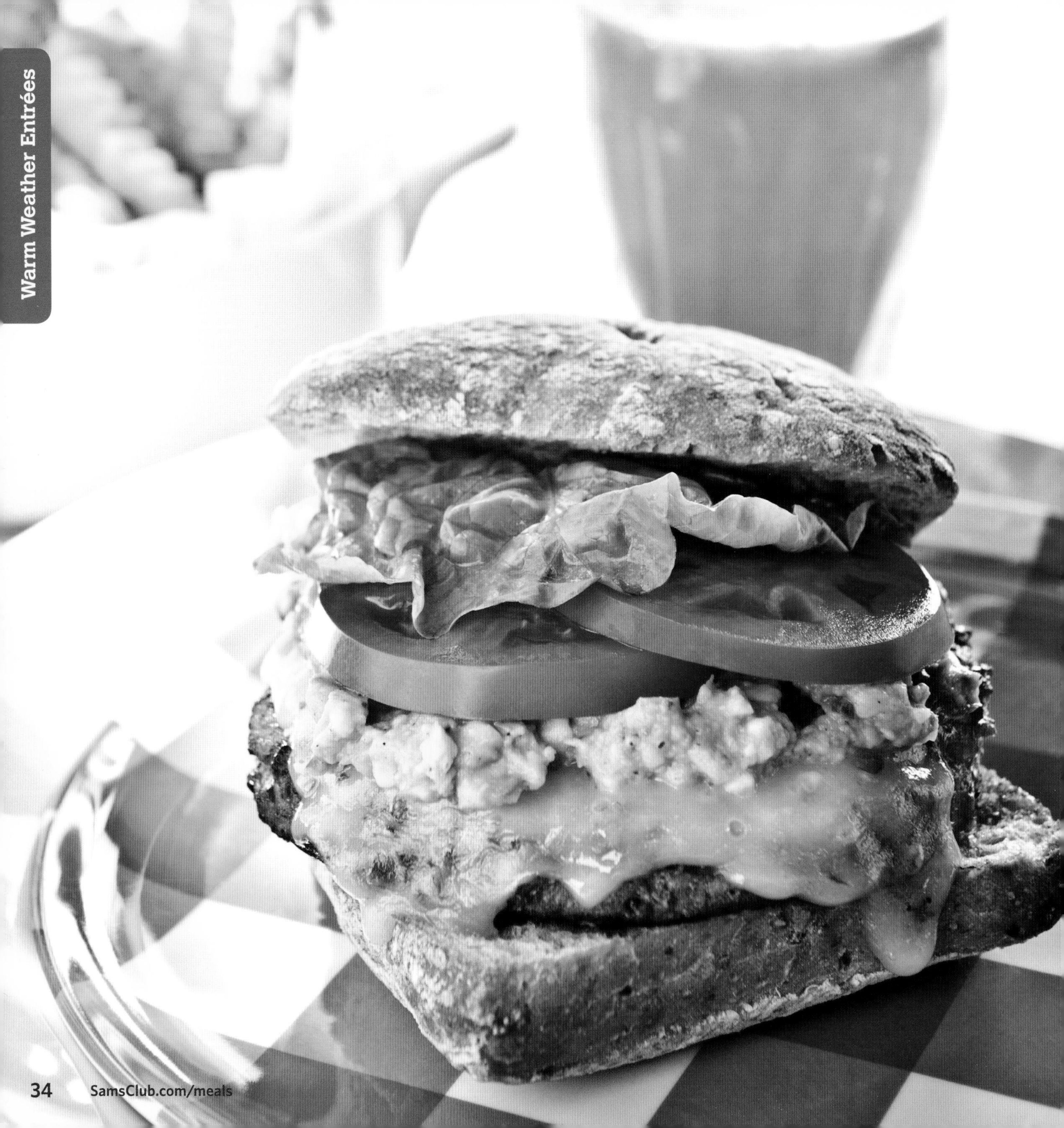

San Diego Cheeseburgers

SoCal and south-of-the-border come together on these hearty, guacamole-topped burgers.

Total time: 30 minutes | Makes 8 servings

Ingredients:

8 frozen Jensen® Sirloin/Beef Burgers

2 ripe avocados, halved, pitted

1 tsp. chili powder

½ tsp. salt

½ tsp. black pepper

1 jalapeño, minced, or to taste

½ cup cilantro, chopped

2 Tbsp. red onion, diced

Juice of ½ lime

8 slices of pepper jack cheese

8 whole-wheat hamburger buns

Tomatoes

Red leaf lettuce

Instructions:

• Preheat grill to medium-low.

• To prepare guacamole, scoop avocado out of peel and place in a medium bowl. Smash until smooth. Add chili powder, salt, pepper and mix, then add jalapeño, cilantro, red onion and lime.

• Grill burgers for 11 to 12 minutes, turning halfway through grill time. Burgers should be cooked thoroughly. The juices should run clear and the center of the burger should not be pink. Cook to an internal temperature of 160°F.

• Place burger on bun bottom. Top with 1 slice cheese, ¼ cup guacamole, tomato, lettuce and bun top.

Use any leftover guacamole with chips as a dip.

Parmesan-crusted Chicken

A new take on traditional chicken Parmesan. Serve with your favorite pasta sauce, if desired.

Total time: 30 minutes | Makes 4 servings

Ingredients:

½ cup Hellmann's® or Best Foods® Real Mayonnaise

¼ cup grated parmesan cheese

4 boneless, skinless chicken breast halves (about 1¼ lbs.)

4 tsp. Italian-seasoned dry bread crumbs

Try making this dish with thin-cut boneless, skinless chicken breasts. Prepare as above, decreasing bake time to 10 minutes or until chicken is thoroughly cooked through.

Instructions:

• Preheat oven to 425°F.

• Combine mayonnaise with cheese in medium bowl. Arrange chicken on baking sheet. Evenly top with mayonnaise mixture, then sprinkle with bread crumbs.

• Bake 20 minutes or until chicken is thoroughly cooked.

Steak Lover's Pizza

You can't top this easy-prep pizza for satisfying hearty appetites.

Total time: 30 minutes | Makes 8 servings

Ingredients:

1 lb. boneless beef sirloin steak

4 tsp. McCormick® Grill Mates® Montreal Steak Seasoning, divided

1 medium onion, sliced into ½" thick slices

1 red or yellow bell pepper, cut into 2" wide strips

1 Tbsp. plus 1 tsp. olive oil, divided

2 cups shredded Monterey Jack cheese, divided

1 lb. fresh pizza dough or frozen dough, thawed
or 1 prepared (12") thin pizza crust

Instructions:

• Sprinkle both sides of steak with 3 teaspoons of the steak seasoning. Brush vegetables with 1 teaspoon of the oil. Grill steak over medium heat 5 to 7 minutes per side or until desired doneness. Grill vegetables 6 to 8 minutes or until tender-crisp. Cut steak and vegetables into bite-size pieces. Mix cheese and remaining 1 teaspoon steak seasoning in small bowl.

• On a lightly floured work surface, roll out dough into a 15" circle. Brush with olive oil. Lay dough onto grill, oil side down. Cover and grill about 3 minutes or until dough is puffed and underside is browned.

• Using tongs, turn pizza over and layer crust with half of the cheese, grilled steak, vegetables and remaining cheese. Close lid. Grill 3 to 4 minutes longer or until cheese is melted and crust is browned. (Check pizza often to avoid burning. Rotate pizza, if necessary.) Slide pizza onto baking sheet. Slice and serve immediately.

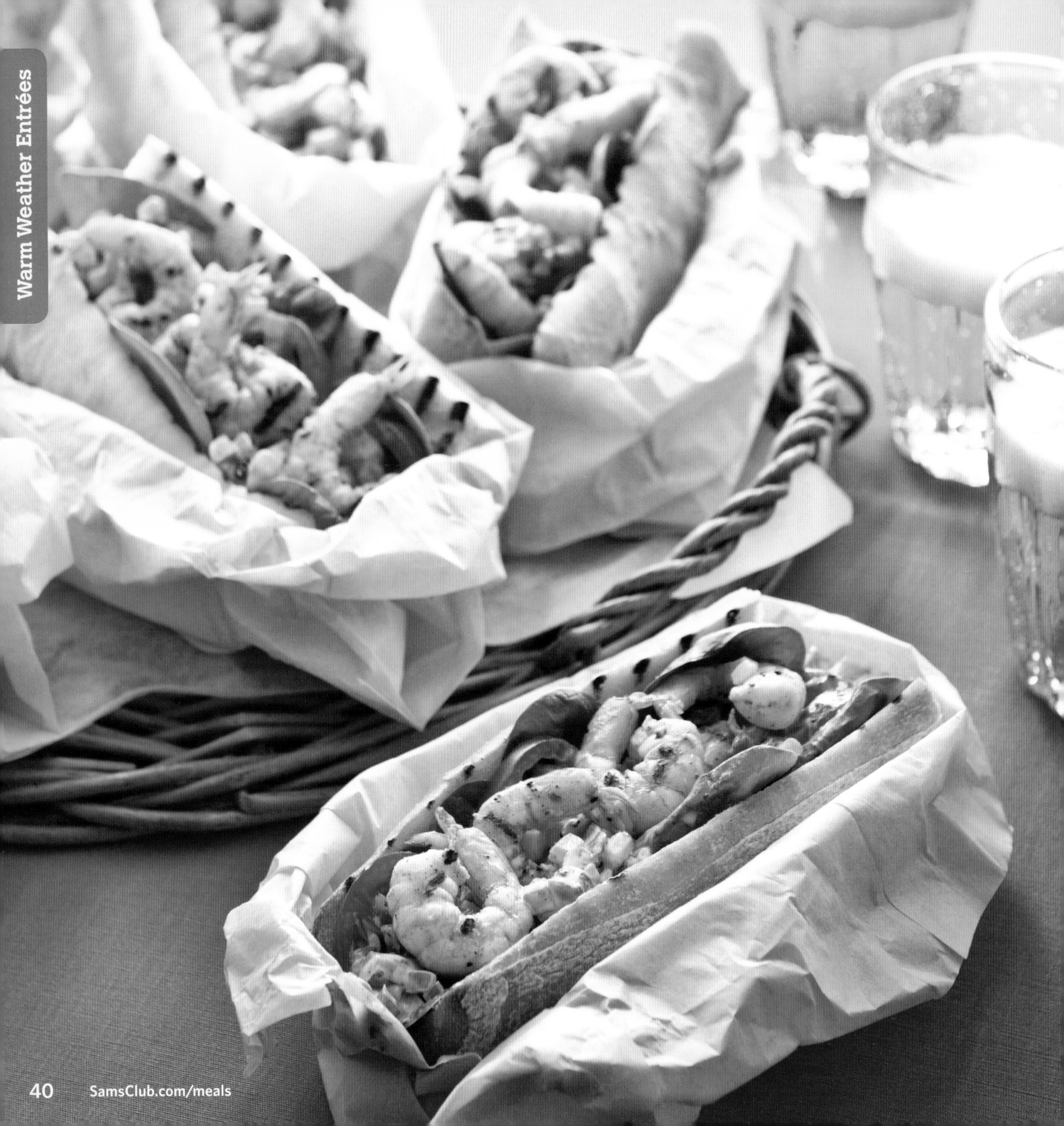

Grilled Shrimp Po' Boy with Grilled Corn Relish

A grilled update on the legendary Louisiana sub sandwich.

Total time: 1 hour, 30 minutes | Makes 8 servings

Ingredients:

8, 6" baguettes or French loaves (grill for added flavor)

2 lbs. Daily Chef™ uncooked 31/40 jumbo shrimp, thawed and tails removed

Grilled Corn Relish

1 ear corn, husk removed

½ large green bell pepper, halved and seeds removed

½ medium red bell pepper, halved and seeds removed

1, 1" slice from a large red onion

½ stalk of celery, chopped finely

½ cup mayonnaise

Shrimp Marinade

½ cup olive oil

6 garlic cloves, chopped fine

2 Tbsp. Old Bay® or cajun seasoning

Juice from 1 lemon

Optional

1 cup of spinach, rinsed and dried

2 medium tomatoes, sliced

1 small red onion, sliced

Instructions:

- For the shrimp marinade, combine olive oil, garlic, seasoning, lemon juice and shrimp. Set aside for at least 10 minutes in the refrigerator.
- Preheat grill to a medium-high heat.
- Drizzle ear of corn, peppers and onion slices with olive oil, sprinkle with salt and pepper and place on grill (approximately 5 to 10 minutes). Turn occasionally and be careful not to burn.
- Once the vegetables have cooled, remove the kernels from the corn and chop the peppers and onion finely.
- Mix all relish ingredients together and place in the refrigerator to cool.
- Place shrimp in grill basket or thread onto skewers and place on the grill and cook for 2 to 3 minutes on each side.
- To assemble the sandwich, divide spinach, tomato and onion among the buns. Spread 2 tablespoons of corn relish on each bun and top with 8-10 grilled shrimp.

Maple-glazed Chicken with Waldorf Salsa

Zesty-sweet chicken is perfectly partnered with a lighter version of the famous fruit salad.

Total time: 45 minutes | Makes 4 servings

Ingredients:

Waldorf Salsa

1 red apple, cored and chopped

1 stalk celery, finely chopped

1 small jalapeño pepper, seeded and finely diced

2 Tbsp. pecans halves, chopped

1 Tbsp. orange juice

1 Tbsp. pure maple syrup

Maple-glazed Chicken

8 chicken thighs (about 3 lbs.)

2 Tbsp. Weber® Kick'N Chicken Seasoning

¼ cup pure maple syrup

Instructions:

• Combine all Waldorf Salsa ingredients in a bowl; set aside in refrigerator.

• Sprinkle seasoning over chicken thighs.

• Grill over indirect medium heat, turning occasionally for 25 to 30 minutes with the lid closed as much as possible, until the chicken is firm to the touch and no longer pink in the center, with an internal temperature of at least 170°F. Brush with ¼ cup maple syrup during the last 5 minutes of cooking.

• Remove chicken from grill and let rest 5 minutes before serving with Waldorf Salsa.

prep time: **20 min.**

Grilled Chicken Paillard with Mushroom Linguine

Mouthwatering and moist—put this dish on repeat for your summer playlist.

Total time: 1 hour, 42 minutes | Makes 4 servings

Ingredients:

24 oz. Classico® Tomato and Basil Pasta Sauce

15 oz. Classico® Roasted Garlic Alfredo Sauce

⅛ tsp. salt

8 small boneless, skinless chicken breast halves (about 2 lbs.)

2 Tbsp. olive oil

2 Tbsp. soy sauce

2 garlic cloves, minced

1 pkg. (16 oz.) linguine pasta

¼ cup unsalted butter

½ cup onion, chopped

8 oz. fresh mushrooms, sliced

1 chicken bouillon cube

2 Tbsp. fresh chives, chopped

2 tsp. fresh parsley, chopped (optional)

2 tsp. fresh thyme, chopped (optional)

Instructions:

• Coat chicken breasts with oil and pound evenly with a mallet to ¼" thickness. Place chicken in a bowl, add soy sauce and garlic and turn until well coated. Cover and marinate in refrigerator for 30 to 60 minutes, turning occasionally.

• Preheat grill to medium heat. Remove chicken from refrigerator, discarding marinade. Grill chicken for 8 to 12 minutes, or until cooked through and internal temperature reaches 165°F, turning occasionally.

• Cook pasta according to package instructions and drain.

• In a large skillet over medium-high heat, cook butter, onion and mushrooms for about 5 minutes, stirring occasionally. Stir in 1 cup of water and bouillon granules, and simmer for 5 minutes or until liquid is reduced by half. Reduce heat to medium and stir in both pasta sauces, chives, parsley and thyme. Simmer for 4 to 5 minutes or until heated through.

• To serve, place hot pasta in a large bowl and toss gently with sauce mixture. Serve one portion of pasta on each plate and top with a grilled chicken breast. Garnish with chopped parsley or chives, if desired.

Brooklyn-style Turkey Burger

Lean, juicy burgers with a New York accent! Feel free to change up the seasonings to add a personal touch.

Total time: 30 minutes | Makes 4 servings

Ingredients:

1 tsp. dried oregano leaves

1 tsp. ground cumin

1 tsp. chili powder

1 lb. Jennie-O Turkey Store® Ground Turkey

1 Tbsp. olive oil

2 medium red onions, thinly sliced

Salt and coarsely ground black pepper, to taste

4 burger buns, split and toasted

4 slices cheddar cheese

Instructions:

• Combine oregano, cumin and chili powder with ground turkey. Form into 4 patties, about ½" thick.

• Heat a skillet sprayed with non-stick cooking spray over medium-high heat. Cook patties in skillet for approximately 18 to 20 minutes, turning 2 to 3 times until internal temperature measures 165°F on a meat thermometer.

• In another skillet, heat oil over medium-high heat. Add onions, salt and pepper. Cook, stirring occasionally, for about 10 minutes or until onions are softened and browned.

• Place turkey patties onto the bottom half of the bun. Top with cheese, onions and top half of buns.

> *Pressed for time? These burgers are also great without the onions. Just top with cheese and your favorite salsa.*

Black and Blue Salmon Salad

A white wine-infused dressing makes this salad a knockout!

Total time: 35 minutes | Makes 4 servings

Ingredients:

4 C. Wirthy & Co.™ Blackened
Salmon portions, thawed

Salad

2 heads romaine lettuce hearts
(approximately 16 stalks)

½ sweet onion

1 large tomato

Dressing

⅓ cup chardonnay (or other white wine)

½ cup heavy cream

¾ cup blue cheese crumbles

Kosher salt and freshly ground black pepper

Extra blue cheese crumbles for topping

Instructions:

• Heat grill to medium-high (approximately 400°F).

• **For the Dressing:** Pour white wine into medium saucepan and cook over medium-high heat, reducing by half. Add the heavy cream and allow it to reduce slightly; add the blue cheese and whisk until smooth. Add salt and pepper to taste. Let dressing cool while cooking salmon.

• **For the Salmon:** Coat grill with cooking spray (or other oil) and place salmon on preheated grill rack; grill 5 minutes per side or until desired doneness.

• **For the Salad:** Remove lettuce stalks from head and rinse, leaving the leaves whole and using only the inner medium-sized stalks. Slice onion into very thin ringlets. Cut tomato into 4 wedges. Arrange 4 lettuce stalks on each plate and place a salmon fillet across the lettuce. Place 3 onion rings on top of each salmon fillet and a tomato wedge next to the fillet. Drizzle with one tablespoon of dressing; garnish with blue cheese crumbles.

Kickin' Chili-rubbed Chicken with Bourbon Peach Glaze

Cedar planks are a delicious, inexpensive way to lend a mild smokiness to grilled meat and seafood. Be sure to soak in water first to prevent burning.

Total time: 55 minutes | Makes 4 servings

Ingredients:

Chicken

6 cedar planks

6 boneless, skinless chicken breasts (4-5 oz. ea.)

2 Tbsp. chili seasoning

Cooking spray

Frozen sliced peaches

Glaze

⅔ cup peach preserves

3 Tbsp. bourbon

1½ tsp. Grand Marnier® or orange juice

1 Tbsp. Lea & Perrins® Worcestershire Sauce

½ tsp. dry mustard

½ tsp. salt

¼ tsp. black pepper

¼ tsp. ground ginger

Instructions:

• Soak cedar planks in warm water for 30 minutes. Preheat grill to medium-high heat.

• Combine glaze ingredients.

• Spray the planks with oil. Rub chicken breasts with chili seasoning blend and place on the planks. Place planks on grill (over direct heat) and baste the chicken.

• Cover with grill lid or tent with aluminum foil.

• Baste chicken with the glaze every 15 minutes. Cook until the internal temperature reaches at least 165°F. Be careful removing the planks from the grill, as the wood pops as it cooks. Serve with grilled peach slices.

Pilgrim's®

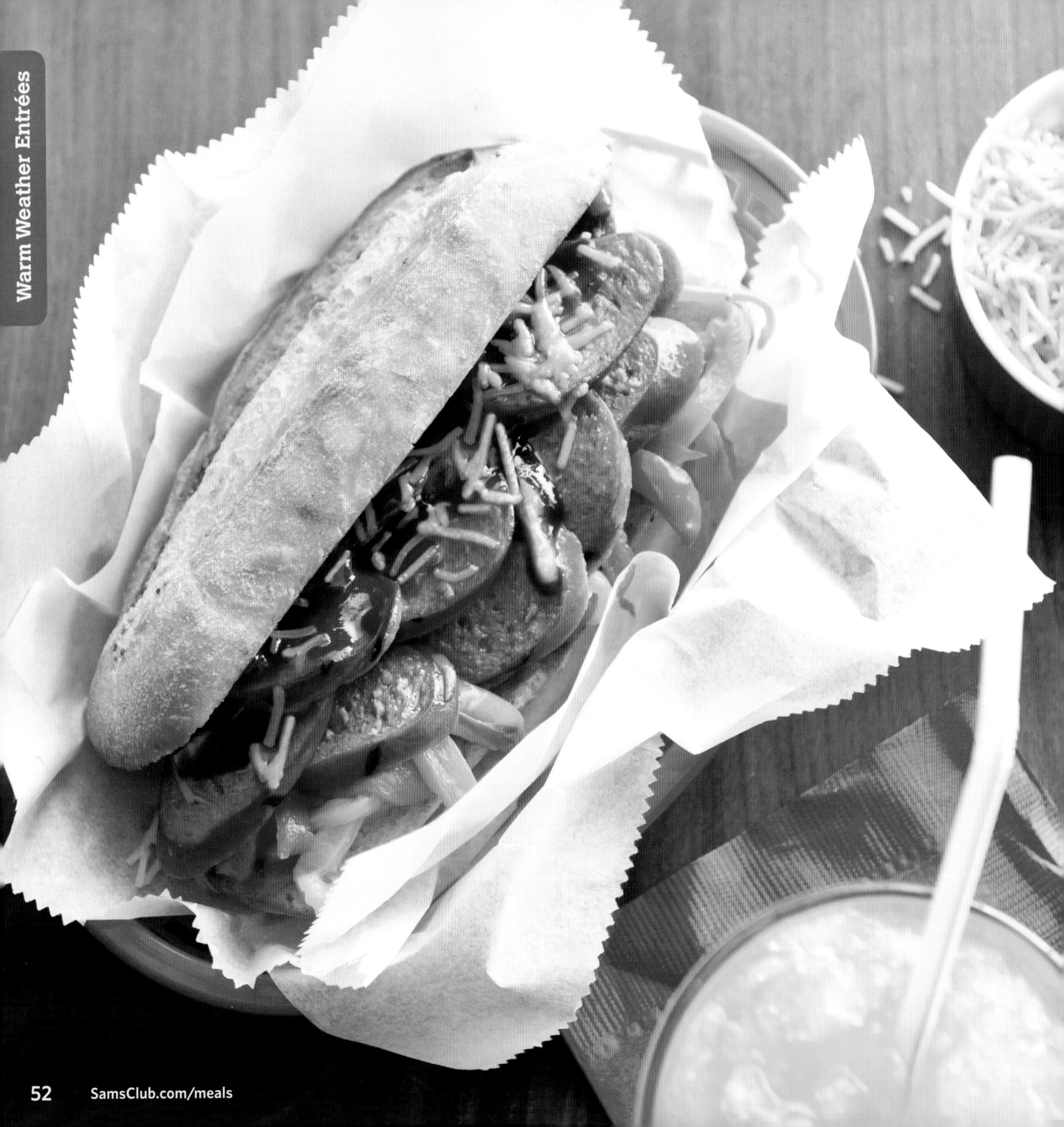

Texas Hold'em High Sandwich

Satisfy your gang with these hearty barbecue sandwiches.

Total time: 25 minutes | Makes 4-6 servings

Ingredients:

2 links Cavanaugh® Smoked Sausage, grilled, thinly sliced

1 French bread loaf, split in half or Texas toast sliced, toasted

½ large red bell pepper, cut into strips

½ large yellow bell pepper, cut into strips

½ cup cheddar cheese, shredded

2 Tbsp. olive oil

¼ cup red onions, diced

1 tsp. Worcestershire sauce

½ tsp. salt

½ cup KC Masterpiece® Barbecue Sauce

Instructions:

• Heat sausage as directed on package and slice thinly.

• In a medium saucepan heat 1 tablespoon olive oil on medium-high and cook bell peppers until tender; set aside. Heat remaining 1 tablespoon oil in the same pan over medium-high heat and cook onions until tender. Add the Worcestershire and salt; cook until almost dry. Stir in barbecue sauce.

• Evenly spread cooked bell peppers on bottom toast. Stack slices of sausage, drizzle barbecue sauce, and sprinkle with cheddar cheese. Place toast on top of stack.

CAVANAUGH.

53

Strip Steak with Onion Wine Sauce

A flavorful wine sauce adds a touch of sophistication to this sizzling steak supper.

Total time: 30 minutes | Makes 4 servings

Ingredients:

2 cups yellow onion wedges, root end removed

1 clove garlic, minced

1 Tbsp. butter or margarine

¼ cup A.1.® Original Steak Sauce®

1 Tbsp. dry red wine

2 beef strip steaks (about 1 lb. total), ¾" thick

Instructions:

• Preheat grill to medium-high heat. Cook onions and garlic in butter in a large skillet on medium-high heat 10 minutes or until onions are tender. Add steak sauce and wine; mix well. Bring to boil.

• Place steaks on grill. Grill 6 to 8 minutes on each side for medium rare (145°F) to medium doneness (160°F). Serve topped with steak sauce mixture.

Summer Barbecue Chicken Pizza

Ranch dressing and barbecue sauce put a tangy spin on this quick-fix homemade pizza.

Total time: 30 minutes | Makes 6 servings

Ingredients:

1 lb. of frozen bread dough, thawed

2 Tbsp. olive oil

½ cup Hidden Valley® The Original Ranch® Dressing

½ cup shredded mozzarella cheese

1 cup bell peppers, sliced (may substitute other vegetable toppings)

1 cup of shredded, cooked Tyson® Boneless, Skinless Chicken Breasts

½ cup KC Masterpiece® Original Barbecue Sauce

Instructions:

• On a lightly floured work surface, roll out dough into a 15" circle. Brush with olive oil.

• Lay dough onto grill, oil side down. Cover and grill about 3 minutes or until dough is puffed and underside is browned.

• Using tongs, turn pizza over and quickly spread with dressing. Scatter cheese, bell peppers and chicken over dressing and cover grill. Grill 2 to 3 minutes or until cheese is melted and underside of pizza is browned.

• Use tongs to slide onto cutting board. Drizzle barbecue sauce on top.

prep time: **10 min.**

Grilled Mediterranean Chicken

These zesty chicken breasts cook up quickly for a savory salad topper or light dinner.

Total time: 22 minutes | Makes 4 servings

Ingredients:

3 tsp. balsamic vinegar

1 Tbsp. olive oil

1½ tsp. Lawry's® Seasoned Salt

1 tsp. dried rosemary leaves, crushed

2 medium tomatoes, cut into ¾" thick slices

4 boneless, skinless chicken breast halves (about 1¼ lbs.)

1 lemon, cut into ¼" thick slices (optional)

Instructions:

• Mix vinegar and oil until well blended; set aside. In a small bowl, mix seasoned salt and rosemary. Brush tomato slices and chicken with vinegar mixture, then sprinkle with seasoned salt mixture.

• Grill chicken over medium heat 5 to 6 minutes per side or until cooked through. Grill tomato slices 2 minutes per side. If desired, grill lemon slices 30 seconds per side. Serve chicken topped with tomato slices. Garnish with lemon slices.

For a quick chicken sandwich, fill pita bread with 1 chicken breast, 2 grilled tomato slices, feta cheese and some romaine lettuce.

LAWRY'S®

Kabobs in a Dash

All the flavor with none of the salt, these savory skewers are ready—and gone—in no time.

Total time: 38 minutes | Makes 4 servings

Ingredients:

2 Tbsp. Mrs. Dash® Original Blend

2 cloves garlic, slivered

1 lb. beef sirloin, cut into 1½" chunks

8 small to medium whole button mushrooms, stems removed

¼ red onion cut into 4 wedges, then cut in half, root end removed

8 cherry tomatoes

Cooking spray

1 Tbsp. olive oil

Instructions:

• In a large bowl, combine Mrs. Dash Original Blend and garlic. Stir together.

• Add the meat, mushrooms, onions and tomatoes to the seasoning blend; toss to coat. Refrigerate for 30 minutes.

• Heat grill or cast iron grill plate. Oil grill grate or spray pan with cooking spray.

• Skewer meat alternating with onion, tomatoes and mushrooms. Brush with olive oil.

• Grill kabobs about 6 to 8 minutes or to desired degree of doneness.

> *Tired of kabob ingredients spinning when you turn the on the grill? Use 2 skewers through all the ingredients (place them about 1" apart). This works especially well for shrimp kabobs.*

Grilled Ahi Tuna Tacos

The sunny taste of the Baja shines in these soft tacos, made with seared, sliced tuna steak and fresh fruit salsa.

Total time: 40 minutes | Makes 4 servings

Ingredients:

4 Treasures from the Sea® Ahi Tuna Steaks, thawed

8 corn tortillas, warmed

Olive oil

Citrus Vinaigrette

¾ cup orange juice

¼ cup lime juice

¼ cup basil, chopped

¼ cup cilantro, chopped

1 Tbsp. honey

1 tsp. salt

¼ tsp. black pepper

½ cup olive oil

Pineapple Pico de Gallo

1 cup chopped pineapple, canned or fresh

½ cup mango, chopped

1 Tbsp. cilantro, minced

1 Tbsp. red onion, chopped

1 Tbsp. lime juice

¼ tsp. salt

Instructions:

• Combine citrus vinaigrette ingredients in one bowl and pineapple pico de gallo ingredients in a separate bowl. Set both aside.

• Brush each side of the tuna steaks with olive oil and grill 2 to 3 minutes per side over high heat. *Medium Rare - cook 4 minutes total. Medium - cook 5 minutes total. Well - cook 6 minutes total.*

• Remove from grill and drizzle with citrus vinaigrette. Let rest about 5 minutes, and then slice the tuna diagonally into ¼" thick slices.

• To assemble tacos, place 2 to 3 slices of tuna on each warmed tortilla and top with pineapple pico de gallo.

Vidalia Onion Chicken

Famous for their natural sweetness, Vidalia onions star in this fast-prep family pleaser.

Total time: 2 hours, 20 minutes | Makes 2 servings

Ingredients:

¾ cup Virginia Brand® Vidalia Onion Vinegarette Salad Dressing

1 Tbsp. lemon juice

2 boneless, skinless chicken breasts (about 1 lb.)

2 Tbsp. butter

¼ cup vidalia onion, diced

1 Tbsp. garlic, chopped

2 cups fresh broccoli

1 cup button mushrooms, sliced

¼ cup Virginia Brand® Vidalia Onion Vinegarette Salad Dressing

Instructions:

• Combine ¾ cup Vidalia Onion Vinegarette and lemon juice in a bowl and add chicken. Marinate at least 30 minutes.

• Preheat an outdoor grill to medium-high heat, slightly oil grate.

• Place marinated chicken on grill and cook 10 to 15 minutes per side, or until no longer pink.

• While chicken is grilling, melt butter in a pan over medium heat. Add onions and garlic, and cook for 3 minutes.

• Add broccoli and mushrooms to the pan and sauté for another 5 minutes.

• Serve grilled chicken along with sautéed vegetables tossed with ¼ cup Vidalia Onion Vinegarette.

Virginia Brand®

Quality Products Since 1962

Grilled Beef Tenderloin with Pan-roasted Potatoes

Mediterranean-style marinated beef and savory spuds—this isn't just any meat and potatoes!

Total time: 1 hour | Makes 4 servings

Ingredients:

1 ½ to 2 lbs. beef tenderloin

¼ cup Bertolli® Classico Olive Oil

1 Tbsp. paprika

1 Tbsp. crushed black pepper

1½ tsp. ketchup

1 tsp. Lea & Perrins® Worcestershire Sauce

1 tsp. mustard powder

1½ tsp. salt

1 Tbsp. rosemary, finely chopped

Potatoes

1½ lbs. baby white or fingerling potatoes

¼ cup Bertolli® Classico Olive Oil

1 tsp. rosemary, coarsely chopped

1 tsp. sage leaf, chopped

1 Tbsp. garlic, chopped

Drizzle

2 Tbsp. Bertolli® Extra Virgin Olive Oil

1 lemon rind, finely grated

1 orange rind, finely grated

Instructions:

• Mix together the Bertolli Classico Olive Oil, paprika, black pepper, ketchup, Worcestershire sauce, mustard powder, salt and rosemary in a small bowl. Pour over tenderloin and let marinate for 1 hour at room temperature.

• Boil potatoes in a large pot of water until they are fork-tender, then strain. In a mixing bowl, combine Bertolli® Classico Olive Oil, rosemary, sage and garlic. Pour the potatoes in the mixing bowl and stir gently with the oil mixture. Place potatoes on top of rectangle made out of 2 pieces of aluminum foil placed on top of each other—this is for added durability on the grill. Seal the sides of the rectangle by folding the edges over. The packet should be able to be turned over with no liquid escaping. Place packet onto grill over direct heat and grill for approximately 30 minutes, turning over once, or until potatoes are nicely browned.

• After the tenderloin has marinated, cook on the grill for 10 to 15 minutes, turning 2 or 3 times to brown on all sides, to desired doneness (medium rare is 145°F). Tenderloin can be placed on grill when potatoes are halfway through cooking. Let the tenderloin rest for 5 minutes then slice into steaks. Combine Bertolli® Extra Virgin Olive Oil and the zest of lemons and oranges; drizzle over tenderloin medallions. Serve immediately alongside the potatoes.

Recipe courtesy of Fabio Viviani, owner and Executive Chef of Cafe Firenze in Moorpark, CA
and Firenze Osteria Italian Restaurant and Martini Bar in Toluca Lake, CA.

New Zealand Rack of Lamb with Grilled Red Pepper-almond Sauce

Impress the eye and the palate with this colorful dish, simple yet fitting for even the fanciest occasion.

Total time: 4 hours, 20 minutes *(includes marinating)* | Makes 2-3 servings

Ingredients:

2 New Zealand Frenched Rack of Lamb (1 pkg.)
2 Tbsp. olive oil
2 tsp. kosher or sea salt
1 Tbsp. black pepper, ground
2 Tbsp. lemon zest

Sauce

2 Italian plum tomatoes, cut in half lengthwise
½ yellow onion, sliced into ½" thick slices
1 red bell pepper, cut in half, lengthwise, seeds removed
2 tsp. ancho chile powder or 1 dried ancho chile

½ cup extra-virgin olive oil
4 Tbsp. almonds, blanched
1 piece slice of white bread, cut into small cubes
3 garlic cloves, chopped
⅛ tsp. cayenne pepper (optional)
½ tsp. smoked Spanish paprika, sweet or hot
1 Tbsp. sherry vinegar or red-wine vinegar
2 Tbsp. water
Kosher or sea salt, to taste
Fresh cracked black pepper, to taste

Instructions:

• Rub lamb racks with olive oil then season with salt, pepper and lemon zest. Refrigerate for 2 hours or overnight. In a casserole baking dish, place tomatoes, pepper, and onion slices in a single layer, drizzle with half of the olive oil and season with salt and pepper, set aside.

• Preheat grill to medium high. Grill tomatoes (seed side first), bell peppers (skin side first) and onion slices until slightly charred, turn over and grill for an additional two minutes. Remove from grill, return to casserole dish, cover with foil and allow to cool slightly.

• Meanwhile, heat a sauté pan over medium-high heat, add ancho chile powder and toast while stirring with a spoon—about 30 seconds. Add olive oil, stir, then add bread cubes, almonds, garlic, smoked paprika, and cayenne pepper and cook until bread is lightly browned. Remove from heat and add sherry vinegar—set aside.

• Peel and seed tomatoes, skin the bell pepper and roughly chop all—place in the work bowl of a food processor or blender. Add almond mixture to work bowl. Add water to sauté pan to loosen any bits and add to work bowl and pulse briefly to blend. Add additional water to thin, if necessary. The sauce will have a slightly coarse texture. Transfer to a serving bowl.

• Place the rack of lamb on grill meat side down (rib bones can be wrapped in foil to prevent burn off). Cook for 18 to 22 minutes turning every 5 minutes—while watching for flare-ups on the grill. When lamb reaches the desired doneness (internal temperature of 135°F for medium rare) transfer to a cutting board, tent with foil and let stand 5 minutes.

• Slice lamb rack between the ribs into chops and arrange on a platter, drizzle with olive oil and serve alongside the pepper-almond sauce.

Recipe provided by Chef Christopher Thompson of The Lamb Cooperative, Wilton, CT.

Sauces, Rubs & Marinades

Chicken

Sauce:

Sweet and Spicy Sauce

Total time: 10 minutes | Makes 2 cups

Ingredients:

½ cup balsamic vinegar

¼ cup soy sauce

¼ cup honey

3 green onions, thinly sliced

1 Tbsp. rosemary, freshly chopped
or 1 tsp. dried

2 tsp. Dijon mustard

Instructions:

• Combine all ingredients in a saucepan and stir
frequently. Bring to a boil and remove from heat.

• Serve warm as a sauce or allow to cool and use
as a marinade.

Recipe submitted by:

Troy Black
Nashville, TN
learn2q.com

As a full-time barbecue competitor, Troy has
had plenty of time to tinker with what makes
a great meal. When preparing an award-
worthy plate, he demands starting with a
perfect piece of meat. To set it apart, he adds
the love: his signature rub, marinade or sauce,
and the proper cooking method.

Rub:
Fiery Lemon Creole Chicken

Total time: 1 hour | Makes 4 servings

Recipe submitted by Elizabeth Nelson

Ingredients:

2 Tbsp. Creole seasoning
2 Tbsp. fresh lemon juice
1 Tbsp. melted butter
1 tsp. ground cumin
4 boneless, skinless chicken breast halves (about 2 lbs.)

Instructions:

- Combine all ingredients except chicken in a small bowl. Rub evenly over chicken and let stand 30 minutes

- Cook chicken on medium-high heat on oiled grill 6 minutes on each side or until done (165°F).

Marinade:
Citrus Marinade

Total time: 2 hours, 10 minutes | Makes 3 cups

Ingredients:

1 cup pineapple juice
1 cup soy sauce
1 cup orange juice
1 Tbsp. ginger, freshly grated
1 Tbsp. garlic, chopped

Instructions:

- Mix together with chicken and marinate at least 2 hours, or longer if preferred.

Use this marinade the next time you make a chicken stir-fry or an Asian chicken salad.

Amick Farms
PREMIUM CHICKEN PRODUCTS

Pork

Sauce:
Eastern Carolina Vinegar Sauce

Total time: 15 minutes | Makes 1½ cups

Recipe submitted by Troy Black

Ingredients:

¼ cup distilled white vinegar

1 cup apple cider vinegar

¼ cup apple juice

2 Tbsp. brown sugar

1½ tsp. kosher salt

½ tsp. fresh ground pepper

¼ tsp. cayenne pepper

¼ tsp. paprika

Instructions:

• Combine all ingredients in a saucepan, stir and bring to a boil. Can be used as a baste for ribs or served over pulled pork at room temperature.

> *Barbecue sauce can be as unique as the region of the country it's from. Traditional Carolina-style barbecue sauce is tangy and vinegar-based, while Kansas City 'cue is sweet tomato-based style. Whatever sauce tickles your ribs, almost all go perfectly with pork.*

Rub:
Chinese-spiced Pork

Total time: 1 hour | *Makes 4 servings*
Recipe submitted by Elizabeth Nelson

Ingredients:

2 tsp. Chinese five spice powder
1 tsp. ground ginger
1 tsp. salt
½ tsp. granulated garlic
¼ tsp. ground red pepper
4 bone-in pork loin chops (about 3 lbs.)

Instructions:

• Combine all ingredients except chops in a small bowl. Rub evenly over chops and let stand 30 minutes.

• Cook chops on medium-high heat on oiled grill 6 to 9 minutes on each side or until done (145°F).

Marinade:
Coconut-lime Marinade

Total time: 2 hours, 6 minutes | *Makes 4 servings*
Recipe submitted by Elizabeth Nelson

Ingredients:

⅔ cup fresh lime juice
⅔ cup coconut milk
¼ cup packed fresh cilantro leaves
¼ cup packed fresh basil leaves
1 Tbsp. ginger root, coarsely chopped
3 small cloves garlic
2 tsp. salt
4 boneless center-cut pork chops (about 1 lb.)

Instructions:

• Process all ingredients except chops in a food processor or blender until smooth, about 10 seconds.

• Place pork chops in a heavy-duty zip-top bag. Pour marinade over chops, tossing to coat. Refrigerate at least 2 hours to marinate.

• Remove chops from marinade and discard. Cook on medium-high heat on oiled grill 6 minutes on each side or until done (145°F).

Seafood

Sauce:
Spicy Pineapple Shrimp

Total time: 50 minutes | Makes 4 servings
Recipe submitted by Mike Chapter

Ingredients:

1 shallot, finely chopped
1 Tbsp. butter
3 Tbsp. apple cider vinegar
Juice and zest of 1 orange
1 can (12 oz.) frozen pineapple juice concentrate, thawed
1 jalapeño pepper, finely chopped
½ tsp. salt
¼ tsp. celery salt
Pinch ground cloves
¼ cup water
1 Tbsp. cornstarch
2 tsp. soy sauce
1 lb. uncooked, peeled and deveined jumbo shrimp with tails on, thawed
Salt and pepper to taste

> *Serve with cilantro rice for a complete meal!*

Instructions:

- Combine shallots and butter in small saucepan; sauté on medium-low heat 5 minutes. Add vinegar and orange juice; bring to boil. Simmer on medium heat 5 minutes, stirring occasionally. Add orange zest, pineapple juice, jalapeño and spices; bring to boil. Simmer on low heat 20 minutes, stirring occasionally.

- Mix water, cornstarch and soy sauce in small bowl until smooth. Stir into juice mixture. Cook 2 to 3 minutes, stirring constantly, until thickened. Remove from heat.

- Thread shrimp onto skewers. Season with salt and pepper. Cook 2 minutes on oiled grill on medium-high heat. Brush with sauce and turn over. Brush with sauce and cook 2 to 3 minutes or until done. Toss or serve with additional sauce.

Rub:
Smoky Tea-rubbed Salmon

Total time: 40 minutes | Makes 4 servings
Recipe submitted by Mike Chapter

Ingredients:

4 green tea bags (about 1 Tbsp.),
opened and emptied into a small bowl

1 Tbsp. brown sugar

1 Tbsp. smoked paprika

1 tsp. kosher salt

½ tsp. garlic powder

¼ tsp. each onion powder, ground cumin, cayenne
pepper and ground thyme

Pinch ground black pepper

4 (5-7 oz. ea.) skinless salmon portions, thawed

Instructions:

• Combine ingredients in a bowl and rub generously
  onto both sides of fish. Let stand 30 minutes.

• Cook fish on medium-high heat on oiled grill 2 to 4
  minutes on each side or until fish flakes easily with fork.

Marinade:
Seafood Marinade with a Kick

Total time: 10 minutes | Makes ¾ cup
Recipe submitted by Troy Black

Ingredients:

⅓ cup extra virgin olive oil

¼ cup fresh-squeezed lemon juice

3 Tbsp. hoisin sauce

½ tsp. fresh garlic, minced

½ tsp. fresh ground black pepper

½ tsp. hot sauce, or to taste

Instructions:

• Combine all ingredients in a plastic zip-top bag and
  mix well. Marinate seafood for 1 to 2 hours and grill.

Beef

Sauce:
Chimichurri Burgers

Total time: 30 minutes | Makes 6 servings
Recipe submitted by Elizabeth Nelson

Ingredients:

¼ cup olive oil
¼ cup red wine vinegar
⅓ cup packed cilantro leaves
⅓ cup packed flat-leaf parsley leaves
¼ cup onion, coarsely chopped
4 cloves garlic
1 jalapeño pepper, seeds and ribs removed
1 tsp. salt
½ tsp. ground black pepper
6 pre-formed 80/20 ground chuck patties or
90/10 ground beef patties, cooked as directed
on package

Instructions:

• Process all ingredients except beef in a small food
  processor until mixture is smooth, about
  10 seconds.

• Serve sauce over prepared burgers.

*Season steaks before you start your
coals or light your grill. This will give the
seasonings a chance to adhere and flavor
the meat without quickly grilling off.*

Rub:
Smoky Chipotle Strip Steak

Total time: 1 hour | Makes 4 servings
Recipe submitted by Elizabeth Nelson

Ingredients:

2 chipotle peppers in adobo sauce, minced
1 Tbsp. vegetable oil
2 tsp. roasted garlic paste
1 tsp. salt
1 tsp. ground cumin
1 tsp. apple cider vinegar
½ tsp. ground black pepper
4 beef strip steaks (about 3 lbs.)

Instructions:

• Combine all ingredients except steaks in a small bowl until well blended. Rub evenly over steaks and let stand 30 minutes.

• Cook steaks on medium-high heat on oiled grill 6 to 9 minutes on each side for medium-rare doneness (145°F).

Marinade:
Beef Marinade

Total time: 2 hours | Makes 1 cup
Recipe submitted by Troy Black

Ingredients:

½ cup balsamic vinegar
¼ cup soy sauce
¼ cup honey
3 green onions, thinly sliced
1 Tbsp. rosemary, freshly chopped
or 1 tsp. dried
2 tsp. Dijon mustard

Instructions:

• Combine all ingredients in a plastic zip-top bag and mix well. Marinate for 1 to 2 hours.

Lamb

Sauce:
Tzatziki Sauce for Lamb Chops

Total time: 1 hour | Makes 4 servings
Recipe submitted by Elizabeth Nelson

Ingredients:

½ cup Greek-style yogurt
½ cup English cucumbers, shredded
3 Tbsp. fresh mint, chopped
1 tsp. lemon zest
2 Tbsp. lemon juice
1 clove garlic, minced
1¾ tsp. salt, divided
8 lamb loin chops (about 2 lbs.)
½ tsp. ground black pepper

Instructions:

• Combine first 6 ingredients and 1 teaspoon salt in a bowl. Refrigerate until ready to serve.

• Sprinkle chops with remaining ¾ teaspoon salt and pepper.

• Cook chops on medium-high heat on oiled grill 6 to 8 minutes on each side for medium-rare doneness (145°F). Serve with prepared sauce.

> *This sauce is also great on a lamb burger.*

Rub:
Curried Lamb Chops

Total time: 1 hour | Makes 4 servings
Recipe submitted by Elizabeth Nelson

Ingredients:

1 Tbsp. brown sugar
2 tsp. Madras curry powder
1 tsp. ground cumin
1 tsp. salt
½ tsp. ground turmeric
8 lamb loin chops (about 2 lbs.)

Instructions:

- Combine all ingredients except chops in a small bowl. Rub evenly over chops and let stand 30 minutes.

- Cook chops on medium-high heat on oiled grill 6 to 8 minutes on each side for medium-rare doneness (145°F).

Marinade:
Kentucky Sweet Bourbon Marinade

Total time: 10 minutes | Makes 1 cup
Recipe submitted by Troy Black

Ingredients:

6 Tbsp. Worcestershire sauce
3 Tbsp. bourbon
3 Tbsp. maple syrup
2 Tbsp. honey-Dijon mustard
2 Tbsp. vegetable oil
¼ tsp. freshly ground pepper

Instructions:

- Combine all ingredients in a plastic zip-top bag and mix well. Marinate for 1 to 2 hours.

Also great with beef.

A Moveable Feast

Chilled Hunt's® Tomato and Vegetable Pasta Salad

An exciting combination of flavors and textures make for a fresh, inviting chilled salad.

Total time: 1 hour, 20 minutes | Makes 9 servings

Ingredients:

12 oz. uncooked rotini pasta (about 4 cups)

1 can (14.5 oz.) Hunt's® Diced Tomatoes, drained

1 cup English cucumber, quartered and sliced

1 pkg. (4 oz.) crumbled feta cheese

3.8 oz. ripe olives, drained and sliced

½ cup shredded carrot

½ cup roasted red pepper, chopped

¼ cup red onion, thinly sliced

1 cup light Italian dressing

¼ cup pine nuts, toasted, optional

Instructions:

• Cook pasta according to package directions, omitting salt. Rinse cooked pasta with cold water. Place in large bowl.

• Add drained tomatoes, cucumber, cheese, olives, carrot, roasted pepper and onion; mix lightly. Add dressing; toss to coat. Cover.

• Refrigerate at least 1 hour prior to serving or until chilled. Sprinkle with pine nuts, if desired.

Citrusy Shrimp Salad

Loaded with shrimp, celery, tomatoes and sweet oranges, turn here for a delicious light lunch or accompaniment to grilled meats.

Total time: 15 minutes | Makes 6 servings

Ingredients:

1 lb. cooked shrimp, peeled and deveined

1 small head Boston lettuce, torn into pieces

1 small head romaine lettuce, torn into pieces

1 cup watercress

1 cup celery, finely chopped

1 small onion, sliced into rings

15 pitted ripe olives, sliced

½ cup Wish-Bone® Italian Dressing

10 cherry tomatoes

2 oranges, peeled and sectioned

Instructions:

• Combine shrimp, lettuces, watercress, celery, onion, olives and Wish-Bone Italian Dressing in large salad bowl; toss well. Add tomatoes and oranges; toss gently.

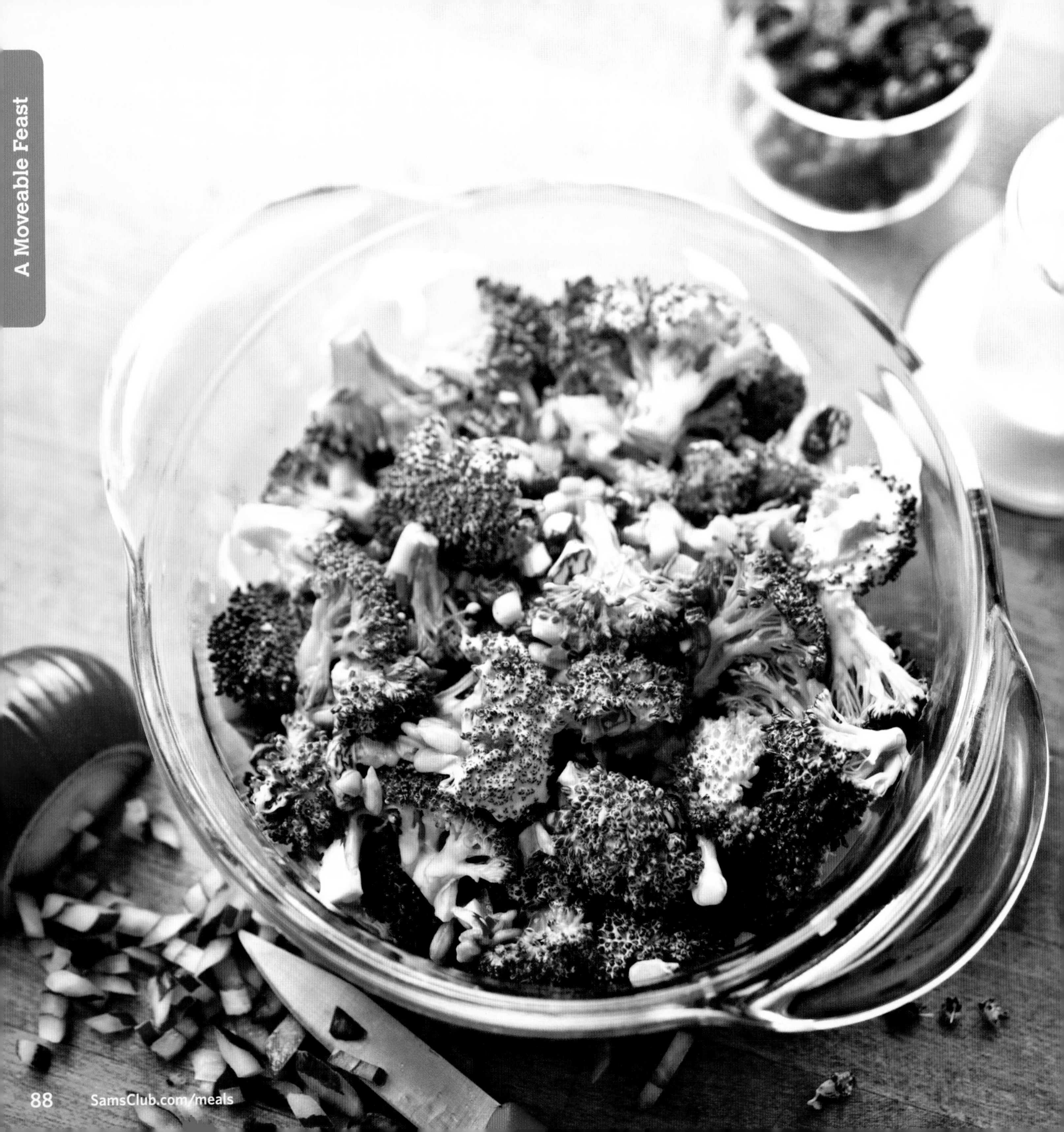

Cool and Crisp Broccoli Salad

Broccoli is tossed with red onion, sunflower seeds and raisins in a light dressing. A perfect summer side dish.

Total time: 10 minutes | Makes 6 servings

Ingredients:

4 cups broccoli or broccolini

¼ cup red onion, finely chopped

2 Tbsp. SPLENDA® No Calorie Sweetener, Granulated

2 Tbsp. cider vinegar

2 Tbsp. light mayonnaise

2 Tbsp. sunflower seeds, roasted and salted

3 Tbsp. seedless raisins

Instructions:

• Discard broccoli stems and cut into florets. Set aside.

• Place remaining ingredients in a medium mixing bowl. Mix well. Add broccoli florets or broccolini. Toss until coated. Chill until ready to serve.

Make this salad extra simple by using bags of pre-washed and pre-cut broccoli.

Summer Squash and Zucchini Pasta Dish

One of summer's most abundant veggies, paired with pasta, prepared sauce and seasonings for a fast and healthful dinner dish in no time.

Total time: 45 minutes | Makes 6 servings

Recipe submitted by:
Lisa LaBarca
Mastic Beach, NY
Member since 2009

The foundation is from my family recipe, but I deviated from it. A little more of this, a little more of that just to make it my own. We started our own garden five years ago, so we always make it fresh.

Ingredients:

2 onions, roughly chopped

2 Tbsp. olive oil

2 yellow squash, cut into 1" pieces

2 zucchini, cut into 1" pieces

4 garlic cloves, chopped

1 tsp. salt

½ tsp. ground black pepper

1 lb. uncooked pasta

1 jar (26 oz.) pasta sauce

3 Tbsp. fresh basil, chopped

1 Tbsp. fresh oregano, chopped

¾ cup Romano cheese, freshly grated

Instructions:

• Sauté onions in hot oil in large skillet on medium-high heat 5 minutes. Add squash, zucchini, garlic, salt and pepper. Cook 20 minutes or until vegetables are tender, stirring occasionally. Meanwhile prepare pasta as directed on package.

• Stir sauce and herbs into vegetable mixture. Cook 5 minutes. Drain pasta; return to pan. Add sauce mixture to pasta; toss well.

• Serve topped with cheese.

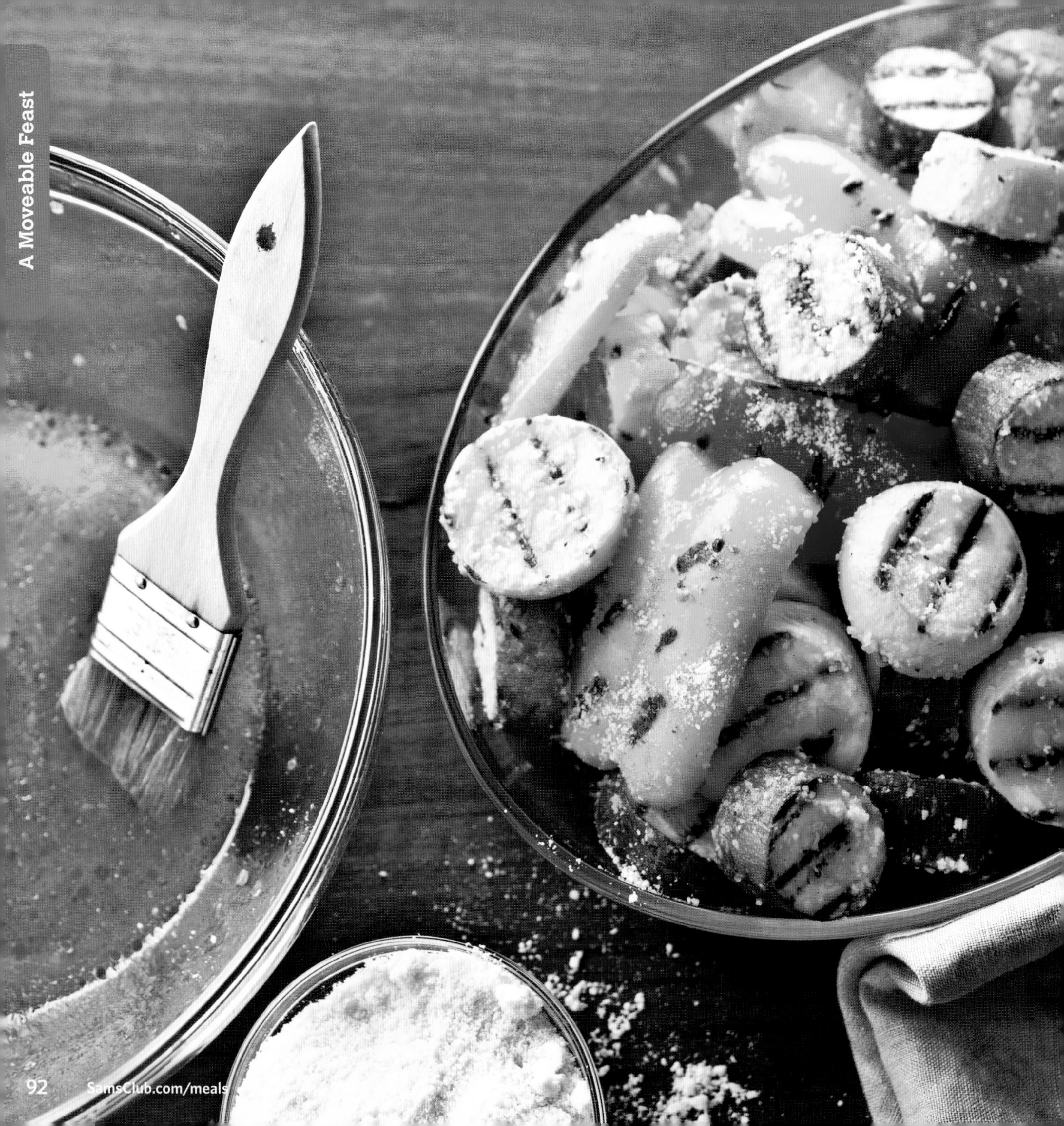

Grilled Parmesan Vegetables

Rich, Italian flavors combine with a classic vegetable medley to create a quick culinary concoction—on a stick.

Total time: 20 minutes | Makes 8 servings

Ingredients:

2 each zucchini and yellow squash, cut into ½" thick slices

2 each red, green and yellow peppers, cut into 1½" wide strips

⅓ cup Italian dressing

¼ cup Kraft® Grated Parmesan Cheese

Instructions:

• Heat grill to medium heat.

• Grill vegetables 10 minutes or until crisp-tender, turning occasionally.

• Place in large bowl. Add dressing; toss to coat.

• Sprinkle with cheese.

Grill these delicious vegetables first. It will free up room on your grill and the flavors blend and develop if they sit for a few minutes before serving. Cover with aluminum foil to help keep them warm. (The aluminum actually steams the vegetables a little and helps them to cook all the way through without burning or getting mushy.)

KRAFT
100% GRATED
PARMESAN
Cheese

Two-bean and Bacon Salad

The robust flavor of bacon and beans with a light, tangy dressing. Great for lunch with warm, buttered rolls or paired with sandwiches.

Total time: 10 minutes | Makes 6 servings

Ingredients:

⅓ cup red onion, finely chopped

2 Tbsp. olive or vegetable oil

2 Tbsp. lemon juice

½ tsp. Dijon mustard

2 medium tomatoes, cut into wedges

1 can (15 oz.) kidney beans, drained, rinsed

1 can (14.5 oz.) Green Giant® Cut Green Beans, drained, rinsed

2.25 oz. ripe olives, drained and sliced

¼ cup crumbled bacon pieces

Instructions:

• In large bowl, stir onion, oil, lemon juice and mustard until well blended.

• Add tomatoes, kidney beans, green beans and olives, gently toss.

• Just before serving, stir in bacon. Cover and refrigerate any remaining salad.

> *Reheat bacon pieces or bits in the microwave prior to serving to help bring out the flavor.*

prep time: **20 min.**

Bacon-stuffed Potatoes

Whole potatoes, grilled and seasoned to perfection with Parmesan cheese and everyone's favorite—bacon.

Total time: 1 hour, 20 minutes | Makes 4 servings

Ingredients:

4 potatoes (about 8 oz. ea.)

¼ cup onion, finely chopped

½ cup Hormel® Bacon Crumbles, divided

¼ cup butter, softened

2 teaspoons seasoned salt

½ cup grated Parmesan cheese, divided

Instructions:

• Prepare grill for direct high heat.

• Slit potatoes at ¼-inch intervals; do not cut all the way through. Wrap in aluminum foil so that the foil can be pulled back to cup the potato (as shown in photo). Grill potatoes 55 to 60 minutes or until almost completely cooked—a knife will be able to go through the slices in the center with little resistance.

• As soon as the potatoes are placed on the grill, combine onion, ¼ cup bacon crumbles, butter, ¼ cup parmesan cheese and seasoned salt in a bowl; mix well. Place mixture in refrigerator to cool.

• Unwrap potatoes rolling foil halfway down the sides. Using a fork to separate the slices, carefully divide the butter mixture between the slices. Combine 2 tablespoons each of the bacon and cheese; sprinkle over the potatoes.

• Return potatoes to grill and heat for 10 minutes or until potatoes are cooked through and butter mixture is melted.

BLT Rotini Pasta Salad

A new twist on two lunchtime classics!

Total time: 25 minutes | Makes 10-12 servings

Ingredients:

1 pkg. (16 oz.) Daily Chef™ Garden Rotini

1 cup mayonnaise

2 Tbsp. white or cider vinegar

½ tsp. salt

¼ tsp. pepper

3 tomatoes, diced

3 green onions, diced

1 pkg. (2.1 oz.) precooked bacon

Daily Chef™: Exceptional quality and value, exclusively from Sam's Club®

New name, same great taste! Daily Chef Gourmet Foods are a delicious, wholesome, budget-friendly choice for everyday meals to special entertaining. All backed by 100% satisfaction guarantee, only from Sam's Club.

Instructions:

• Cook pasta according to package directions; drain and rinse with cold water. Place in large salad bowl.

• Combine mayonnaise, vinegar, salt and pepper in a small bowl and stir until blended. Pour over pasta and stir to coat evenly.

• Add tomatoes and green onions.

• Cook bacon according to package directions in microwave oven until crisp; crumble and add to salad. Stir all ingredients together.

Life is Sweet

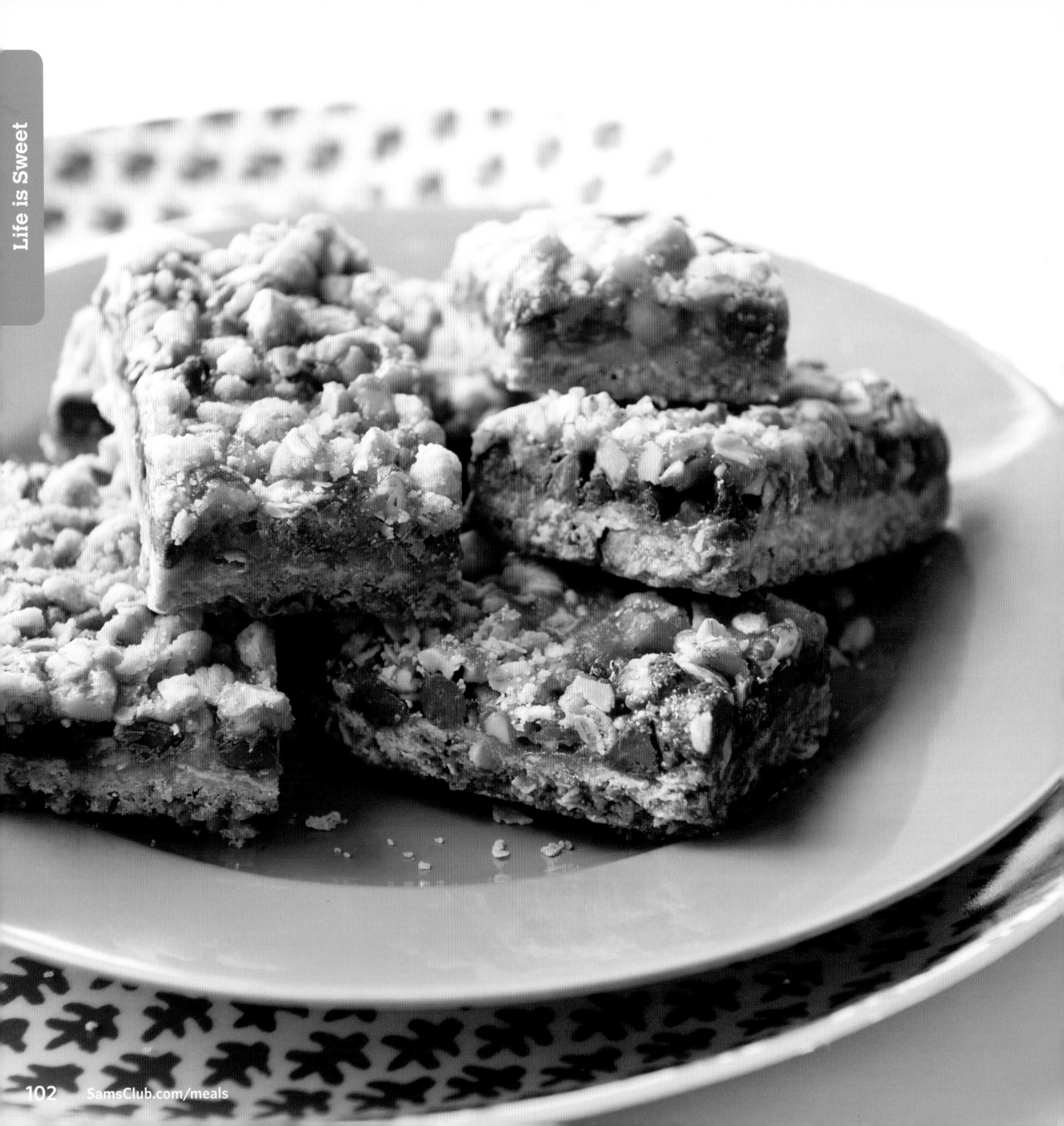

Caramel Oatmeal Chewies

Gooey, chocolaty and packed with the goodness of oats, this caramel-topped bar is a sweet ending to everything from picnics to potlucks.

Total time: 37 minutes | Makes 30 bars

Ingredients:

1¾ cups Quaker® Oats (quick or old fashioned, uncooked)

1¾ cups all-purpose flour, divided

¾ cup firmly packed brown sugar

½ tsp. baking soda

¼ tsp. salt (optional)

12 Tbsp. (1½ sticks) butter or margarine, melted

2 cups semi-sweet chocolate chips

1 cup nuts, chopped

1 cup caramel ice cream topping

Instructions:

• Heat oven to 350°F. Grease bottom of 13x9" metal baking pan.

• In large bowl, combine oats, 1½ cups flour, brown sugar, baking soda and salt. Stir in butter; mix well. Reserve 1 cup oat mixture; press remaining oat mixture onto bottom of baking pan.

• Bake 12 to 15 minutes or until golden brown. Sprinkle with chips and nuts. Mix caramel topping with remaining flour in small bowl; drizzle over nuts to within ¼" of pan edges. Sprinkle with reserved oat mixture. Continue baking 18 to 22 minutes or until golden brown. Cool in pan on wire rack; refrigerate until firm. Cut into bars.

Millionaire Pie

You don't have to be rich to enjoy this indulgent dessert that whips up quickly with simple ingredients.

Total time: 2 hours | Makes 2 pies, 8 servings each

Ingredients:

1 can (14 oz.) sweetened condensed milk

¼ cup lemon juice

29 oz. crushed pineapple, drained

11 oz. mandarin oranges, drained

1 cup nuts (such as walnuts or pecans), chopped

1 tub (16 oz.) Cool Whip® Whipped Topping, thawed

2, 9" graham cracker pie crusts

Instructions:

• Combine first 5 ingredients in large bowl. Gently stir in whipped topping.

• Spoon into crusts. Refrigerate or freeze 2 hours or until firm.

For individual servings, spoon filling into small cups or ramekins. Top with crumbled graham cracker crust.

Recipe submitted by:
Paula McMullen
Karthaus, PA
Member since 2001

It is easy to make, it tastes good, it's affordable and makes you feel like you don't need anything else in the world! My kids just love the filling and prefer not to have the crust. I've made it for large crowds and I use Dixie Cups, put a tablespoon of graham crackers in the bottom, fill the rest up with the filling and they keep frozen until you need them.

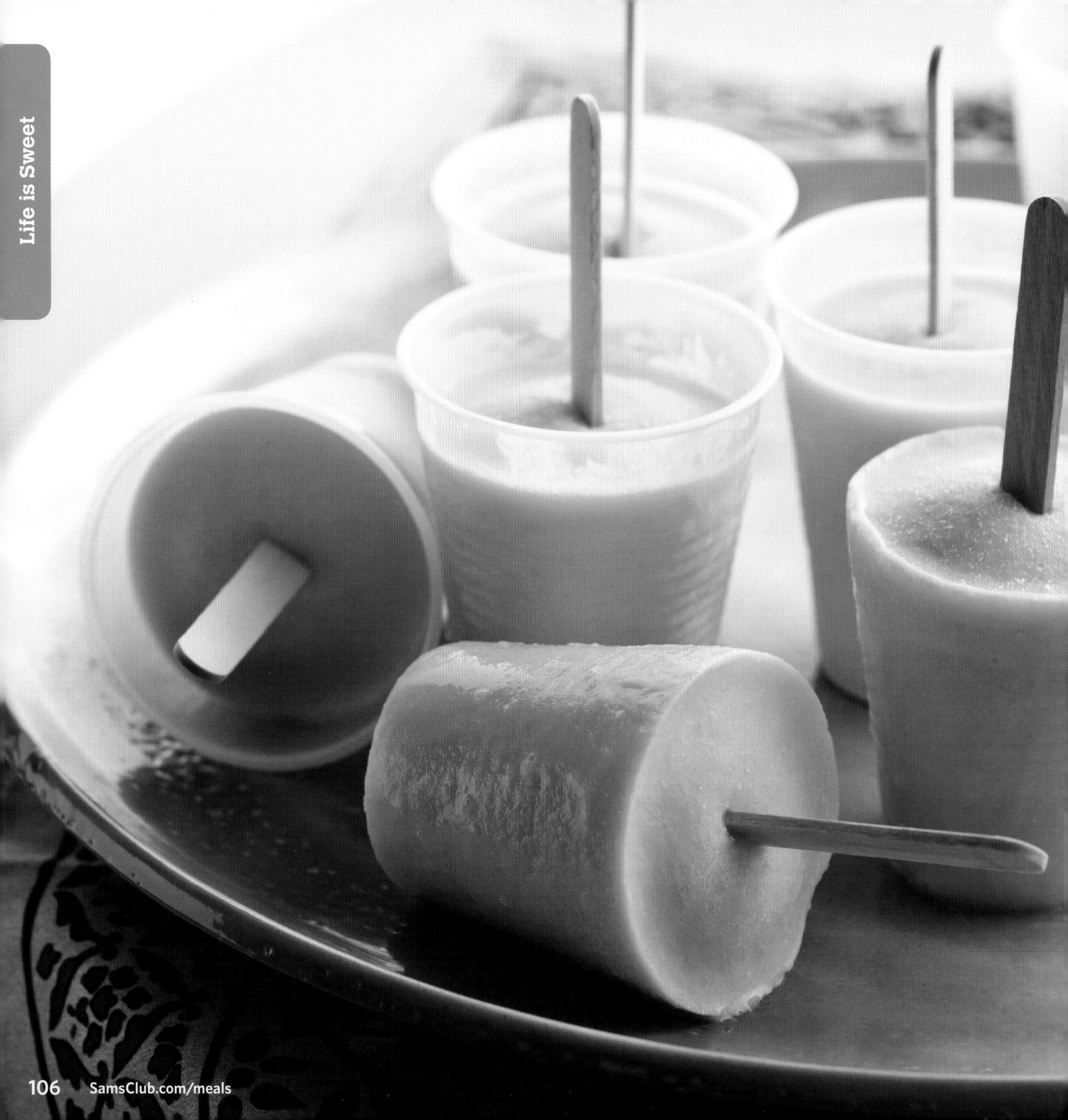

Peach Yogurt Pops

Fun, festive and full of summer fruit flavor with the tang of real yogurt.

Total prep time: 5 minutes; Freeze until firm | Makes 8 servings

Ingredients:

1 can (15 oz.) Del Monte® Lite Yellow Cling Sliced Peaches

6 oz. (1 container) low-fat vanilla yogurt

8 (4 oz.) plastic or paper drink cups

8 wooden popsicle sticks or plastic spoons

Instructions:

• Pour undrained fruit into food processor or blender container. Cover and purée.

• Add yogurt; blend until smooth.

• Pour into cups; freeze until partially frozen.

• Place stick in center of each cup.

• Return to freezer and freeze until firm (several hours/overnight).

Bubbly Berries with Lemon Sorbet

Sorbet and lemon-lime soda team up to make a fruity, fizzy frozen treat.

Total prep time: 1 hour; Chill-to-serve time: 2-3 hours | Makes 4 servings

Ingredients:

3¼ cups Simply Lemonade®

2 cups Sprite®

1 cup fresh blackberries

¾ cup fresh blueberries

1 cup fresh raspberries

1 cup fresh strawberries, quartered

1½ cups fresh mint leaves, cleaned and trimmed

Instructions:

- Make sorbet by placing lemonade in a saucepan over medium-high heat and reducing to 1⅔ cups, about 20 to 25 minutes. Cool and chill well. Place in an ice cream machine and process according to manufacturer's instructions. When partially frozen scrape into a chilled metal bowl and freeze for several hours or overnight.

- Place the soda in a saucepan over medium-high heat and reduce to ¾ cup, about 15 minutes. Cool slightly and add the berries and half of the mint leaves. Cover, cool completely, and chill for several hours or overnight.

- Ladle berries and syrup into chilled serving bowls. Top with sorbet and garnish with mint leaves.

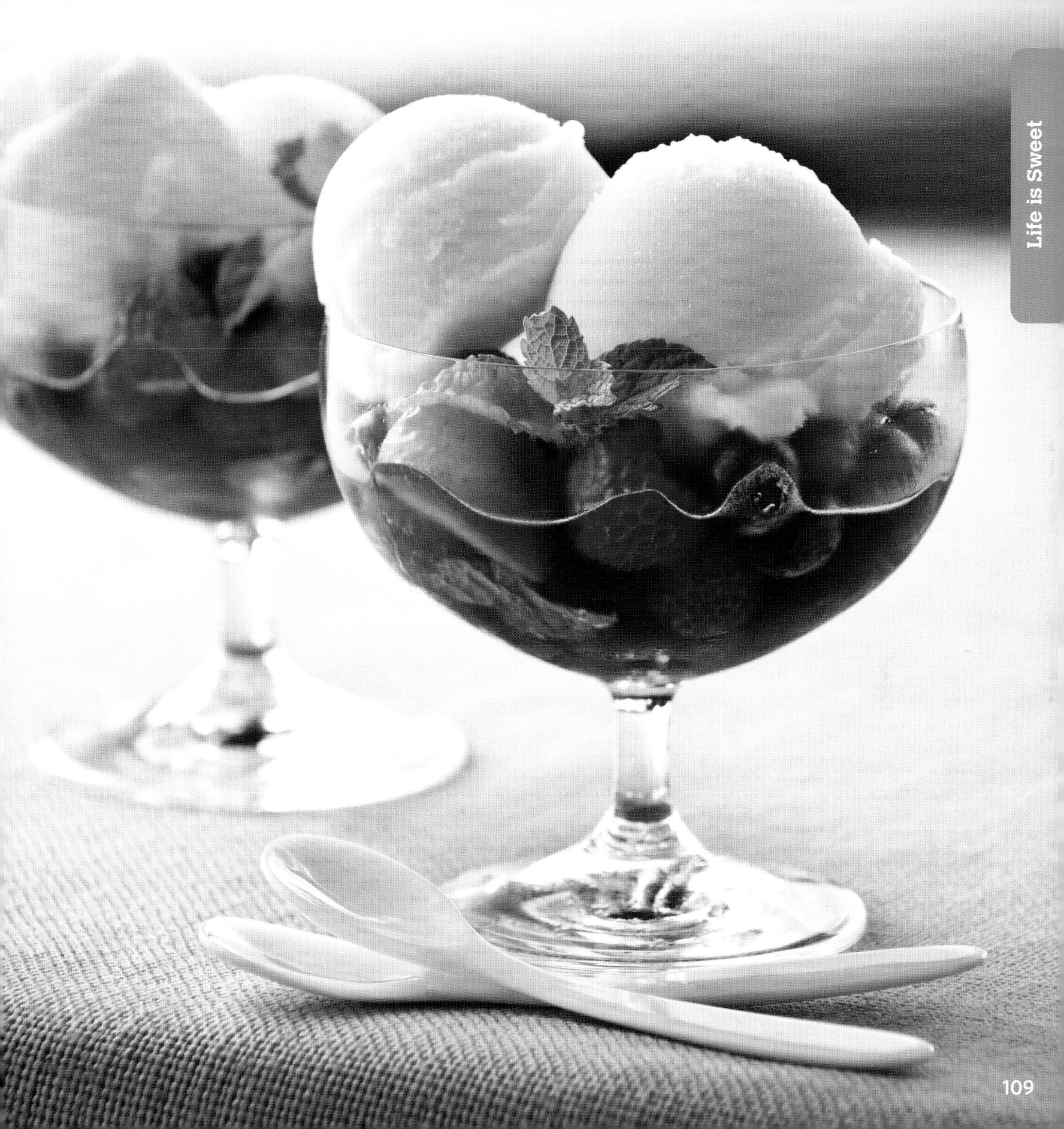

Orange Dream Supreme Cake

White cake mix makes a delicious substitute for orange in this sunny citrusy dessert.

Total time: 1 hour, 5 minutes | Makes 12 servings

Ingredients:

Cake

1 pkg. orange supreme cake mix

1 pkg. (3.4 oz.) instant vanilla pudding

4 eggs

1 cup orange soda

¼ cup vegetable oil

Glaze

1 cup prepared whipped cream cheese icing or vanilla frosting

1 tsp. orange extract

Instructions:

• Heat oven to 325°F.

• **For Cake:** Combine all ingredients in mixer bowl. Beat with electric mixer 3 minutes. Pour into a nonstick Bundt cake pan sprayed with cooking spray. Bake 38 to 40 minutes or until a toothpick inserted in cake comes out clean. Cool in pan 15 minutes. Invert onto wire rack. Cool completely before frosting.

• **For Glaze:** Microwave icing and extract in microwaveable bowl 10 seconds. Stir until smooth. Drizzle over cooled cake.

Recipe submitted by:
Brenda Covert
Greer, SC
Member since 1991

My daughter and I love Dreamsicle-flavored anything! What's great about this is that it can be made in the microwave. I had seen a recipe for a chocolate microwave cake with Coke in the batter. That's what gave me the idea to create an orange/vanilla microwave cake with orange soda in it, and it came out perfect!

Want a sweet treat but tight on time? Make it in the microwave! Prepare cake ingredients per the recipe, pour into lightly greased microwave-safe Bundt pan. Cover batter with wax paper, microwave on low for 10 minutes, then increase to medium and cook 6 to 7 minutes or until set. Let cake stand uncovered 15 minutes, invert onto a plate.

Chocolate Chip Cupcake Scoops

These two dessert classics collide to create a new favorite with kids of all ages.

Total time: 1 hour | Makes 12 servings

Ingredients:

12 oz. semi-sweet chocolate chips

12 small scoops of Breyers® Natural Vanilla Ice Cream

Instructions:

• Line 12-cup muffin pan with aluminum foil cupcake liners, discarding paper part of liners; set aside.

• Microwave chocolate chips in medium microwave-safe bowl on high, stirring occasionally, 1½ minutes or until smooth.

• Spoon chocolate by rounded tablespoonfuls into muffin liners, then use the back of the small spoon to spread chocolate to completely coat sides and bottoms.* Refrigerate 30 minutes or until firm.

• Carefully peel and discard foil from chocolate cups. Arrange chocolate cups on dessert plates. Fill each with 1 scoop Breyers Ice Cream, then garnish, if desired, with sliced fruit, cookies, mini chocolate chips and/or sprinkles.

* If remaining chocolate in bowl becomes too thick to spread, microwave on HIGH 10 to 20 seconds to thin; stir well. Do not microwave foil.

> *Make cupcake sundaes by topping each cup with your favorite ice cream topping, whipped cream and a cherry!*

Cranberry Chocolate Cheese Bars

Tart, sweet and neat to eat. This makes a big batch, for smiles all around.

Total time: 1 hour | Makes 36 bars

Ingredients:

1 cup Ocean Spray® Craisins® Original Dried Cranberries

1 cup (2 sticks) butter or margarine, softened

1 cup firmly packed brown sugar

2 cups all-purpose flour

1½ cups quick or old-fashioned oats

2 tsp. orange peel, grated

2 cups semi-sweet chocolate morsels

1 pkg. (8 oz.) cream cheese, softened

1 can (14 oz.) sweetened condensed milk

Instructions:

• Preheat oven to 350°F. Grease a 13x9" baking pan.

• Beat butter and brown sugar in large mixer bowl until creamy. Gradually beat in flour, oats and orange peel until crumbly. Stir in morsels and Craisins; reserve 2 cups mixture. Press remaining mixture onto bottom of prepared baking pan.

• Bake for 15 minutes. Beat cream cheese in small mixer bowl until smooth. Gradually beat in sweetened condensed milk. Pour over hot crust; sprinkle with reserved flour mixture. Bake for additional 25 to 30 minutes or until center is set. Cool in pan on wire rack. Cut into bars.

prep time: **15 min.**

Frozen Pear Pops

Chill out with this homemade, real fruit-filled version of everyone's favorite dessert on a stick.

Total time: 3 hours | Makes 10 servings

Ingredients:

3 cups chopped Del Monte® Canned Pear Halves

⅔ cup reserved light syrup from pears

2 Tbsp. sugar

Juice from 1 lemon

2 tsp. 100% pure vanilla extract

Pinch sea salt

Instructions:

• Purée all ingredients in blender until smooth.

• Pour into freezer pop molds (or use disposable cups and sticks); freeze 3 hours or until firm.

Recipe submitted by:
Deborah Rosen
Pennsboro, WV
Member since 2007

I had an old Italian recipe for pineapple popsicles and just wanted to try something different. With the pears, I use less sugar than the old recipe and I just added the vanilla.

prep time: **10 min.**

Coolers & Quenchers

Granola Strawberry-banana Smoothie

Total time: 5 minutes | Makes 2 servings

Ingredients:

2 containers (6 oz. ea.) Yoplait® Original Strawberry Yogurt

½ cup 2% milk

½ cup fresh strawberries, halved

1 banana, sliced

4 Nature Valley® Oats 'n Honey Granola Bars

Instructions:

- In blender, place yogurt, milk, strawberry halves and banana slices. Break up 3 granola bars; add to blender. Cover and blend on high speed 10 seconds. Scrape sides.
- Cover and blend about 20 seconds longer or until smooth.
- Pour into 2 glasses. Crumble remaining bar; sprinkle in each glass.
- Garnish top of each smoothie with fresh strawberries. Serve immediately.

Summer Cranberry Spritzer

Total time: 10 minutes | Makes 8 servings

Ingredients:

40 oz. Ocean Spray® Cranberry Juice Cocktail, chilled

½ cup fresh lime juice

2 cans (12 oz. ea.) regular or diet lemon-lime carbonated beverage

Instructions:

- In 2-quart nonmetal pitcher, combine juices; mix well. Stir in carbonated beverage. Serve over ice.

Patriotic Tea Punch

Total time: 1 hour, 10 minutes | Makes 4 servings

Ingredients:

4 cups water
2 cups cranberry or pomegranate juice
⅓ cup Lipton® Lemon Iced Tea Mix
1 medium red delicious or gala apple, sliced
1 cup small strawberries, halved leaving hulls intact
1 cup fresh blueberries

Instructions:

• In pitcher, combine water, juice and Lipton® Lemon
  Iced Tea Mix. Add fruit; chill 1 hour or until ready
  to serve. Serve over ice and garnish, if desired, with
  additional skewered fruit and mint.

Lemonade Fruit Cooler

Total time: 10 minutes | Makes 4 servings

Ingredients:

2 cups water
½ cup Country Time® Lemonade Flavor Drink Mix
3 cups seedless watermelon, chopped
1 cup ice cubes

Instructions:

• Place all ingredients in blender; cover.
  Blend on high speed until smooth.
  Pour into four glasses to serve.

Frozen Bloody Mary

Total time: 5 minutes | Makes 4 servings

Ingredients:

1 liter regular V8®
2 tsp. horseradish sauce
1 Tbsp. Worcestershire sauce
2 stalks celery
1 Tbsp. TABASCO® Sauce

> *You can also garnish with pickled okra, carrots and lime.*

Instructions:

- Fill blender with ice, add all ingredients, blend and serve.

- Garnish glasses with a pinch of black pepper and pickled green beans.

Orange Mint Tea

Total time: 5 minutes, plus time for tea to brew | Makes 8 servings

Ingredients:

2 qts. Lipton® Iced Tea
(follow directions on package)
1 bunch fresh mint
3 Navel oranges, sliced

Instructions:

- Add mint leaves and orange slices to tea and let sit overnight.

Strawberry Agua Fresca

Total time: 2 hours, 10 minutes | Makes 8 servings

Ingredients:

2 pints hulled strawberries
¼ cup sugar
1 qt. water

Instructions:

• Blend strawberries and sugar until smooth
  in blender.

• Mix strawberry/sugar mixture with water in pitcher
  or serving container.

• Chill for at least 2 hours or serve over ice.

• Garnish with strawberries.

Honey-berry Soda

Total time: 4-6 hours for ice cubes; 5 minutes
for the drink | Makes 8 servings

Ingredients:

2 pints blueberries
¼ cup water
2 Tbsp. honey
Ice cube trays
1 liter ginger ale

Instructions:

• Blend blueberries, honey and water until smooth
  in blender.

• Fill ice cube trays with blueberry mixture and freeze.

• Add two blueberry ice cubes to serving glass and
  top with ginger ale.

123

From our partners:
A few of our favorite tips

Sam's Club® extends a sincere thank you to our valued contributors who helped make this cookbook possible. From these trusted brands, a collection of delightfully new and delectably tried-and-true tips to inspire and enjoy.

National Pork Board: Fresh pork in sealed packaging can be safely stored in the refrigerator at 40°F or lower for up to four days after purchase prior to cooking, or up to six months in the freezer when wrapped airtight.

Jennie-O Turkey Store®: Did you know Jennie-O ground turkey is all natural, low fat and gluten-free? Enjoy as you would ground beef grilled as burgers, or brown and season to use in tacos, on nachos and in casseroles.

Jensen Sirloin Burger: Perfect for the grill, skillet or broiler, simply cook these flavorful burgers right from the freezer, turning when patties become soft on first side. Cook until internal temperature of meat is at least 160°F.

Pilgrim's Pride® Chicken Breast: Marinades are a delicious way to make sure chicken stays moist and flavorful on the grill. Lightly scoring each breast crosswise before marinating helps ingredients penetrate better and cook more evenly.

New Zealand Lamb: For the most tender, flavorful eating experience, allow cooked lamb to rest at room temperature under loosely wrapped foil for 10 to 15 minutes before carving. Slicing meat against the grain will also produce superior texture.

Wish-Bone® Italian Dressing: Want to dress up chicken in an instant? Marinate 2 pounds skinless, boneless breasts in 1 cup of Wishbone Italian Dressing for 30 minutes and toss on the grill until cooked through.

Hormel® Bacon Crumbles: Nothing kicks up ordinary corn muffin mix like bacon! Prepare as directed on the package, stirring in ½ cup bacon crumbles and ⅓ cup of your favorite shredded cheese before baking. Try it for breakfast, too!

Hunt's® Diced Tomatoes: Diced tomatoes are a tasty, convenient topping for salads, in soups, and a tropical salsa-in-minutes mixed with chopped fresh onion, peppers, cilantro, and pineapple or mango.

Bertolli® Olive Oil: Bertolli Olive Oil enhances the natural flavors of food. Bertolli Classico is ideal for grilling with its mild profile. Then drizzle grilled meats or fish with Extra Virgin for a robust, full-bodied flavor as you sauté savory sides with Extra Light Tasting.

Tyson® Cavanaugh Sausage®: Slice into ¼" rounds and serve in a fondue pot or slow cooker with prepared barbecue sauce for a quick and easy appetizer.

Del Monte®, Lite Yellow Cling Peaches: A taste of summer is never far with Del Monte peaches! Slice on garden salads for a splash of color and hint of sweetness; blend with low-fat milk, ice and a dollop of fruit yogurt for an instant smoothie.

Byron's® Pulled Pork: Need a barbecue fix fast? Keep Byron's BBQ Pulled Pork on hand for delicious sandwiches, and as a smoky-sweet topping on baked potatoes, nachos and pizza.

KRAFT® Mexican Shreds: Don't settle for the same old sandwich! Spread 2 tablespoons refried beans on a flour tortilla; top with fresh shredded lettuce, fresh chopped tomato and KRAFT Mexican Style Finely Shredded Four Cheese. Roll up and enjoy!

DOLE® Pineapple Chunks: Pineapple is a delicious way to add a hint of sweetness and a healthy dose of nutrition to all your favorite recipes. Simply skewer pineapple and grill along with your favorite meat and veggies for a sweet twist on traditional kabobs.

Amick Farms: Our all-natural chicken breasts are perfect for a quick, delicious meal anytime, and stocking up can be a real time-saver. Simply divide into family-size portions and seal well with plastic wrap then aluminum foil. Label, date and freeze for up to 6 months. Always thaw in the refrigerator; allow about 5 hours per pound of boneless chicken pieces.

Hellmann's® Mayonnaise: Hellmann's is a deliciously simple way to keep poultry moist and flavorful. Adding mayo to boneless, skinless chicken breast (as in the Parmesan-crusted Chicken recipe on Page 36) helps keep it moist and delicious.

McCormick® Grill Mates® Seasoning: Transform regular food into grilled masterpieces. Shake on Grill Mates Montreal Steak Seasoning, a robust blend of coarsely ground peppers, garlic and spices for bolder tasting steaks and burgers. Master the flame. Master the flavor.

Weber® Seasoning: Serve a great tasting meal any night with Weber Kick'N Chicken Seasoning. Sprinkle on chicken breasts and grill until done. Generously season strips of chicken and use to make delicious fajitas, lettuce wraps or taco salads.

Lawry's® Seasoned Salt: The original seasoned salt. A unique blend of salt, spices and herbs that tastes great on prime ribs, steaks, chicken and casseroles. The possibilities are endless.

Mrs. Dash®: Out of the cupboard and onto the table: Pour Mrs. Dash into a spice or pepper grinder, and keep it with the salt and pepper shaker for meals. The sodium-free and easy way to add zest to steaks, veggies, pasta and more.

Daily Chef™ Uncooked Jumbo Shrimp: For perfectly grilled shrimp shish kabobs, use two skewers together to hold shellfish in place and allow for even cooking.

Quaker® Oats: Add fiber and flavor to your baking when you add oats into the mix. Taste the delicious difference with the recipe for Caramel Oatmeal Chewies on Page 103.

Hidden Valley Ranch®: You love it in salads, but this convenient dry mix also makes a zesty rub for pork and chicken, adds zip to soups and stews, and lends kick to our crowd-pleaser Fiesta Dip, Page 24.

A.1.® Steak Sauce: Use A.1. Steak Sauce to beef up all of your meals. It's delicious on eggs, potatoes and stirred into soups and chili for an extra zing!

KC Masterpiece®: Try barbecue sauce to give a tangy new twist to old favorites. Add to your favorite meatloaf recipe with a cup of shredded cheese for a kick. Or use it to create an appetizer that will please any palate by mixing with grape jelly, heating in a chafing dish or slow cooker and serving with meatballs.

Unilever®, Breyers® Natural Vanilla Ice Cream: Pair scoops with grilled peaches, apricots or plums. Drizzle with warm caramel or fudge sauce for a sweet and satisfying warm-weather treat.

Treasures from the Sea®, Ahi Tuna: For best cooking results, Ahi Tuna should be removed from its packaging and thawed in the refrigerator overnight. Once thawed it can be seasoned and grilled or pan seared for a healthy meal in minutes. You can also cut into cubes and skewer with your favorite fruits and vegetables for a new twist on kabobs.

KRAFT® 100% Grated Parmesan: Try these quick crisps with spreads and dips: make 1 tablespoon mounds of grated cheese on a lightly greased cookie sheet. Flatten tops with the back of a spoon and bake at 300°F on the middle rack for 5 to 6 minutes or until golden. Cool on paper towel before serving.

Coca-Cola®: Did you know marinating in soda adds tenderness and a hint of sweetness to your favorite meat? Taste it for yourself with a delicious recipe for Coca-Cola Chicken Wings on Page 20.

SPLENDA® Sweeteners: SPLENDA® No Calorie Sweetener is a sweet alternative for sugar when baking! Just measure and pour, 1 cup sugar = 1 cup SPLENDA® No Calorie Sweetener, Granulated. It's an easy way to lower your sugar and calorie intake and still enjoy your favorite treats.

KRAFT® Country Time Lemonade: Add a sunny twist to white cake mix with three tablespoons of lemonade powder. Prepare as directed; serve with whipped topping or ice cream for a cool citrusy-sweet treat.

Simply Lemonade®: Have family fun and help give back with a free lemonade stand. Take donations instead of payments, and let the kids deliver the proceeds to a local charity.

General Mills®, Green Giant® Cut Green Beans: In a small bowl, toss well-drained green beans with prepared Italian dressing to taste. Chill. Serve as a savory topping on salad, or a quick-fix side dish for grilled meats.

Unilever®, Lipton® Lemon Iced Tea Mix: For a tangy cool-down treat when it's warm outside, prepare iced tea according to package instructions, pour into ice pop molds and freeze until firm. Sure to be a poolside hit!

C. Wirthy & Co.™: Did you know ocean-farmed salmon is an excellent source of high-quality, affordable protein? Serve it blackened, teriyaki-style, in burgers or on salads for a healthy meal that's as satisfying as it is simple to prepare.

Vita Food Products Vidalia Onion Vinegarette Dressing: For a refreshing salad, combine 32 oz. packaged coleslaw or broccoli slaw mix with 16 oz. Vidalia Onion Vinegarette. Toss with 8 oz. dried cranberries and 2 cups shelled pistachios. Chill at least 1 hour before serving.

Ocean Spray®, Craisins®: Naturally fat-free, cholesterol-free and sodium-free, dried cranberries are a neat-to-eat treat and a good source of fiber. Great in summer salads, cereal, yogurt toppings and baking.

Ocean Spray® Cranberry Juice Cocktail: Try cranberry juice to add a splash of summertime sparkle to fruit-based cocktails, mocktails and soft drinks. Serve with a twist of lime, lemon, orange or a sprig of fresh mint.

Classico® Tomato & Basil Pasta Sauce: Explore a new way to enjoy Classico with this creative dip that's ready in minutes. Combine equal parts of sour cream and Classico Tomato & Basil Pasta Sauce in a bowl; blend in grated Parmesan cheese, ground pepper and oregano to taste. Serve warm or cold with pita chips, crackers or thin breadsticks.

Daily Chef™ Garden Rotini produced by American Italian Pasta Co.®: For a more flavorful noodle, add a pinch of salt to boiling water during cooking. Drain immediately when done and rinse with cool water to keep it from sticking together. Before serving, return cooked pasta to pot, toss in sauce to coat. Transfer to bowl before serving.

General Mills, Yoplait® Original Strawberry Yogurt and Nature Valley® Granola Bars: Try Yoplait Light for a quick and healthy snack. Crumble in a Nature Valley Granola bar for a satisfying yet low-fat breakfast to go.

Index

Index